Pattern Discrimination

IN SEARCH OF MEDIA

Götz Bachman, Timon Beyes, Mercedes Bunz,
and Wendy Hui Kyong Chun, Series Editors

Pattern Discrimination

**Clemens Apprich, Wendy Hui Kyong Chun,
Florian Cramer, and Hito Steyerl**

IN SEARCH OF MEDIA

University of Minnesota Press
Minneapolis
London

meson press

In Search of Media is a joint collaboration between the
University of Minnesota Press and meson press, an open
access publisher, https://meson.press/

Published by the
University of Minnesota Press, 2019
111 Third Avenue South, Suite 290
Minneapolis, MN 55401-2520
https://www.upress.umn.edu

in collaboration with
meson press
Salzstrasse 1
21335 Lüneburg, Germany
https://meson.press

ISBN 978-1-5179-0645-0 (pb)
A Cataloging-in-Publication record for this book is available
from the Library of Congress.

Contents

Series Foreword

"Media determine our situation," Friedrich Kittler infamously wrote in his Introduction to *Gramophone, Film, Typewriter.* Although this dictum is certainly extreme—and media archaeology has been critiqued for being overly dramatic and focused on technological developments—it propels us to keep thinking about media as setting the terms for which we live, socialize, communicate, organize, do scholarship, et cetera. After all, as Kittler continued in his opening statement almost thirty years ago, our situation, "in spite or because" of media, "deserves a description." What, then, are the terms—the limits, the conditions, the periods, the relations, the phrases—of media? And, what is the relationship between these terms and determination? This book series, *In Search of Media,* answers these questions by investigating the often elliptical "terms of media" under which users operate. That is, rather than produce a series of explanatory keyword-based texts to describe media practices, the goal is to understand the conditions (the "terms") under which media is produced, as well as the ways in which media impacts and changes these terms.

Clearly, the rise of search engines has fostered the proliferation and predominance of keywords and terms. At the same time, it has changed the very nature of keywords, since now any word and pattern can become "key." Even further, it has transformed the very process of learning, since search presumes that, (a) with the right phrase, any question can be answered and (b) that the answers lie within the database. The truth, in other words, is "in there." The impact of search/media on knowledge, however, goes beyond search engines. Increasingly, disciplines—from sociology to economics, from the arts to literature—are in search of media as a way to revitalize their methods and objects of study. Our current media situation therefore seems to imply a new term, understood as temporal shifts of mediatic conditioning. Most broadly, then, this series asks: What are the terms or conditions of knowledge itself?

To answer this question, each book features interventions by two (or more) authors, whose approach to a term—to begin with: *communication, pattern discrimination, markets, remain, machine*—diverge and converge in surprising ways. By pairing up scholars from North America and Europe, this series also advances media theory by obviating the proverbial "ten year gap" that exists across language barriers due to the vagaries of translation and local academic customs. The series aims to provoke new descriptions, prescriptions, and hypotheses—to rethink and reimagine what media can and must do.

Introduction

Clemens Apprich

By now, the fact that social networks create "echo chambers" has become a truism. As we know from Greek mythology, *Echo,* the loquacious mountain nymph, was condemned to repeating phrases—as a punishment for helping Zeus hide his many affairs from Hera. Rejected by Narcissus, she wasted away until nothing but an echo remained. Narcissus in turn—as punishment for his many cruel rejections—fell in love with his own image and then killed himself, a victim of unrequited love. Hence, one may conclude, the inability to respond to others makes reciprocal exchange impossible and isolates the individual. In a narcissistic culture of self-affirmation, fostered by algorithmic personalization, communality—if not democracy—allegedly has been destroyed. But this analogy misses a deeper implication of the sociotechnical transformation. Concealed behind the "echo chambers" and "filter bubbles" of social media is an incredibly reductive identity politics, which posits class, race, and gender as "immutable" categories. Hence, at a time in which Western democracies have become "postracial" and vocal conservative and liberal-progressive critics within the humanities have declared studies of race/class/gender/sexuality passé, identity has returned with a vengeance—that is, if it ever left.

To understand the kinds of identity politics enabled by network technologies, this book examines a fundamental axiom of computational cultures: pattern discrimination. While the word *discrimination* originates from the Latin verb *discriminare,* where it simply

x   means "to separate, to distinguish, or to make a distinction," it was in the late nineteenth century that it became overtly political. In parallel to the development of racist ideology, discrimination since then has referred to a prejudicial treatment of individuals based on a social category (e.g., race, gender, sexuality, age, class). However, in different terminologies the original meaning of the term has been preserved. This is why in computer science "pattern discrimination" is still used as a technical term to describe the imposition of identity on input data, in order to filter (i.e., to discriminate) information from it. But far from being a neutral process, the delineation and application of patterns is in itself a highly political issue, even if hidden behind a technical terminology. The point of this book is to trace and uncover the implicit ties between the ideological and technical uses of discrimination, as we can experience it in algorithmically enhanced systems of pattern recognition.

What would happen if we took discrimination with regard to data-driven politics seriously and built systems that acknowledged the fundamental fluidity of identity? What would happen if network science and Big Data met critical theory? In her essay, Hito Steyerl offers a taste of what this could mean. She shows us the hardwired ideologies of a machinic vision, in which data builds the basis of our reality. However, this reality doesn't necessarily match with the catchphrases of the data industry. Rather than a smooth operation, algorithmically enhanced pattern recognition struggles with a massive amount of real—that is, dirty—data. As Steyerl explains, algorithms must constantly fix the mess that we call life. And just like in real life, the criteria to decide what to include and exclude are intrinsically political. But then why is it that there is almost no discussion about the implicit racist, sexist, and classist assumptions within network analytics? How, in other words, can we have a serious debate about Big Data and pattern discrimination if most people (or their data) are either blanked or don't really care? This is the question Florian Cramer tackles in his text by contrasting computer analytics with classical hermeneutics. Instead of a narrative function based on syntax, computers employ statistical

methods, thereby leaving behind older concepts of critical interpretation. But since data is never pure and analytics never fully
objective, interpretation—and thus hermeneutics—recurs through
the back door of computational analytics. In this sense, allegedly
"old" concepts of the humanities may give us a key to the enigma
of pattern discrimination: "interpretation," "meaning," "identity,"
or "subjectivity" are well-explored terms that can and should be
taken into account when it comes to a better understanding of our
digitized and networked world.

That our world is currently remodeled by network science as the
science of neoliberalism is the central observation of Wendy Hui
Kyong Chun. In her piece she dissects the concept of homophily,
which grounds the breakdown of seemingly open and boundless
networks into a series of poorly gated communities, a fragmentation further fostered by the agent-based market logic embedded
within most capture systems. If networks segregate, it is because
network analyses rest on and perpetuate a reductive identity
politics, which posits race and gender as "immutable" categories
and love as inherently "love of the same." Her point is neither to
dismiss nor to villainize network science; rather, the article calls for
more interdisciplinary intersections, so that we can understand the
"performative" nature of networks in all the senses of the word:
they both enact what they describe and create their alleged subject
via repetitious acts.

In his concluding piece, Clemens Apprich takes up the epistemological problem of pattern discrimination on the basis of new ways
of perception, representation, and knowledge that are generated
by the shift from mass media to social media. The transition from
one media system to another, he argues, creates a set of paranoid
effects, which can be read as the attempt to adapt to this change.
Beyond the colloquial understanding of paranoia, Apprich's text
refers to its productive moment, when the subject, after having
experienced a rupture in the symbolic order, tries to reappropriate
reality. In times of Big Data, when our traditional patterns of
interpretation have no real bite anymore, we must ask how the

"paranoid thinking machine" can be put to different ends, in order to reconstitute the world.

The articles collected in this volume do not deny that Big Data, machine learning, and network analytics constitute a new authority—after the divine and the rational. But they do plead for a certain serenity, for a strategic step back to not get caught in the narcissistic admiration of our own image. Because this is what digital cultures ultimately are: the reflection of our own lives—messy, beautiful, and unjust.

A Sea of Data: Pattern Recognition and Corporate Animism (Forked Version)

Hito Steyerl

What is recognition? Remember the famous primordial scene of (self)-recognition described by Louis Althusser: a policeman hails someone in the street yelling "Hey you!" In that moment the person is supposed to recognize himself both as subject ("you") and as subjected to the policeman's authority ("hey!"). "Hey you!" is the primary formula of social control, the most basic pattern of personal and political recognition. The categories of knowledge, control, and privilege are established with one single gesture (Althusser 1971, 163).

But today the situation is more complicated. Gone are the days when it was about one person walking down the street. It's not five, five thousand, or even five million people crossing the street but 414 trillion bits, the approximate amount of data traveling the internet per second. Imagine the policeman standing there trying to yell: "hey you!" at every single one of them. It must be flabbergasting. On top of that he has to figure out whether they are sent by a spam bot, a trader, a porn website, a solar flare, Daesh, your mum, or what. Imagine Althusser's scenario of recognition translated to this reality and you get this desperate plea for assistance: "Developers, please help! We're drowning (not waving) in a sea of data—with data, data everywhere, but not a drop of information" (Sontheimer 2015). This quote is part of a series of texts called "Signal v. Noise" posted to the NSA's internal website from 2011 to 2012. Its author complains of an overload of intercepted data: "It's not about the data or even access to the data. It's about getting information from the truckloads of data . . ." (Sontheimer 2015). In the NSA's description, data are an overwhelming ocean, more landscape than library, more raw material than focused message, more taken than givens. Secret services randomly siphon off "truckloads" of data. But the sheer volume of traffic becomes a source of bewildering opacity. This problem is not restricted to secret services however. Even WikiLeak's Julian Assange himself has said, "We are drowning in material" (Sontheimer 2015).

Pattern Recognition

This is where pattern recognition comes into play. The NSA columns' main question is how to extract a signal from the noise of excessive data. The answer is: by "discovering patterns in large data sets" (Wikipedia 2017a). This happens via: "the analysis of large quantities of data to extract previously unknown, interesting patterns" (Wikipedia 2017b) like dependencies, clusters, or anomalies. Althusser's overwhelmed cop gets thrown a lifeline. The people he was supposed to hail are now patterns of life extracted from geolocation data, phone records, social media trawling, and online shop cookies. They are subjected to continuous surveillance by governments, corporations, their own cars, and Barbie dolls. It's now a question of defining flocks, swarms, rhythms, and constellations within the deafening noise of intercepted data. But how exactly to separate signal and noise, or maybe rather how to define them in the first place?

Jacques Rancière tells a mythical story—or maybe let's call this kind of story a political fable—about how this might have been done in ancient Greece. How did people distinguish signal from noise back then? Sounds produced by affluent male locals were defined as speech, whereas women, children, slaves, and foreigners were assumed to produce garbled noise. The distinction between speech and noise served as a kind of political spam filter. Those identified as speaking were labeled citizens and the rest as irrelevant, irrational, and potentially dangerous nuisances. Similarly, today, the question of separating signal and noise has a fundamental political dimension. Dividing signal and noise means not only to "filter" patterns but also to create them in the first place. What does an "anomaly" exactly mean in pattern "recognition"? As with the gesture of Althusser's cop, "recognition" creates subjects and subjection, knowledge, authority, and as Rancière adds, neatly stacked categories of people. Pattern recognition is, besides many other things, also a fundamentally political operation.

In 1988 Fredric Jameson declared paranoia to be one of the main cultural patterns of postmodern narrative, pervading the political unconscious.[1] According to Jameson, the totality of social relations could not be culturally represented within the Cold War imagination—and the blanks were filled in by delusions, conjecture, and whacky plots featuring Freemason logos (Jameson 2009, 15). Today, however, apophenia replaces paranoia.[2]

How is this? After Edward Snowden's leaks, one thing became clear: many conspiracy theories were actually true (cf. Sprenger 2015). Worse, they were outdone by reality. Post-Snowden, any speculation about hidden plots or guesswork about intrigue and unlawful behind-the-scenes activities became outdated. One didn't have to speculate anymore about conspiracy; there was evidence to prove it. This does not mean there is no more secrecy. There is. But the same structural conditions that allow ubiquitous surveillance— leaky and unevenly regulated information architectures—also continue to benefit bottom-up exposure—which on the other hand could be totally fake. Potentially all information—at least a lot of it—is removed from the control of its authors once digitally transmitted; any piece of information can and likely will become public at some point in time, regardless if it is factual or not—and more often, it's not. The only paranoia that still makes sense is pure reality: a scenario deemed vastly unlikely by all but some experts has become actual.

Additionally Jameson's totality—the sum of social relations—has taken on a different form. It is not absent; on the contrary, it is rampant. Totality has returned with a vengeance in the form of oceanic "truckloads of data." Social relations are distilled as contact metadata, relational graphs, infection-spread maps, or just a heap of fake news.

This quantified version of social relations is just as readily deployed for police operations as for targeted advertising, for personalized clickbait, eyeball tracking, and proprietary feed algorithms. It works both as social profiling and commodity form. Kloutscore-based A-list, black ads marketing, and presidential kill list are based on similar proprietary operations. Today totality comes as probabilistic notation that includes your fuckability as well as disposability ratings, not to mention precise estimates of your skin color. It catalogues affiliation, association, addiction; it converts patterns of life into death by Hellfire missile.

This type of totality is also the necessary counterpart of messianic expectations of singularity. Singularity—the pet myth of Californian ideology—describes a time when artificial intelligences take over.

According to Jameson, singularity is also characteristic of a period in which general rules no longer apply.[3] It's case by case instead; or rather, every case for itself. Singularity is a California fantasy of *Weltgeist,* this time riding a Lethal Autonomous Weapons System enabled by spontaneous jurisdiction, a scarce rule of law, and SKYNET metadata. However, the real singularity of our times is most obviously the semi-divine mythical entity called the markets, a set of organizations regarded as both autonomous and super-intelligent, of such providence, by the way, beautiful providence, that human reasoning has to bow to its vast superiority. This is the real-existing singularity in our times, an entity allegedly endowed

with a superhuman intelligence that can under no circumstances
be questioned.

The corresponding totalities are taken care of by apophenia and pattern recognition. Pattern recognition formulas sift through truckloads of humble and seemingly trivial data sets divined from the entrails of online shopping and massively multiplayer online gaming.[4] No interaction is too modest or menial to be scanned, stored, and saved for eternity. A singularity in which every case is unique correlates to a totality governed by probability management.

If paranoia was a standard Cold War narrative, apophenia happens when narrative breaks down and causality has to be recognized— or invented—across a cacophony of spam, spin, fake, and gadget chatter.

This is also reflected in contemporary paradigms of truthfulness. The five W questions of traditional inquiry—who, what, where, when, and why—have been replaced with the seven V's of Big Data processing: velocity, variety, volume, veracity, variability, visualization, and value. Veracity is no longer produced by verifying facts. It's a matter, as one big-data expert put it, to cleanse "'dirty data'" from your systems[5] (Normandeau 2013). So what are dirty data? Here is one example:

> Sullivan, from Booz Allen, gave the example the time his team was analyzing demographic information about customers for a luxury hotel chain and came across data showing that teens from a wealthy Middle Eastern country were frequent guests.
> "There were a whole group of 17 year-olds staying at the properties worldwide," Sullivan said. "We thought, 'That can't be true.'" (Kopytoff 2014)

The data was thus dismissed as dirty data, before someone found out that, indeed, it was true. Brown teenagers, in this worldview, are likely to exist. Dead brown teenagers? Also highly probable.

But rich brown teenagers? This is so improbable that they must be dirty data and cleansed from the system! The pattern emerging from this operation to separate noise and signal is not very different from Rancière's political noise filter for allocating citizenship, rationality, and privilege. Affluent brown teenagers seem just as unlikely as speaking slaves and women in the Greek polis. Had the researchers uncovered that seventeen-year-old brown teenagers were likely to be shot dead by police at their properties they wouldn't have flinched but rather worked on a targeted email campaign promising discounts for premium demise.

Probability enters truth production on an extensive scale with the unsurprising effect that the patterns supposed to be uncovered in massive data correspond to some degree with the patterns that are already assumed to be found there. On the other hand, though, dirty data are something like a cache of surreptitious subaltern refusal; they express a refusal to be counted and measured:

> A study of more than 2,400 UK consumers by research company Verve found that 60% intentionally provided wrong information when submitting personal details online. Almost one quarter (23%) said they sometimes gave out incorrect dates of birth, for example, while 9% said they did this most of the time and 5% always did it.[6] (Cabrera 2015)

Dirty data is where all your and my refusals to fill a constant onslaught of online forms accumulate. Everyone is lying all the time, whenever possible, or at least cutting corners. Not surprisingly, the most "dirty" area of data collection is consistently pointed out to be the (U.S.) health sector. Doctors and nurses are singled out for filling out forms incorrectly, sometimes even going as far as to abbreviate "gpa" for "grandpa," a move that deeply baffles and confounds data-mining operations. It seems health professionals are just as enthusiastic about filling forms for systems that are supposed to replace them as consumers are to perform clerical work for corporations that will spam them in turn.

In his book *The Utopia of Rules* David Graeber gives a profoundly
moving example of the forced extraction of data. After his mom
suffered a stroke he went through the ordeal of having to apply for
Medicaid on her behalf.

> I had to spend over a month not long after dealing with
> the ramifying consequences of the act of whatever anon-
> ymous functionary in the New York Department of Motor
> Vehicles had inscribed my given name as "Daid," not
> to mention the Verizon clerk who spelled my surname
> "Grueber." Bureaucracies public and private appear—for
> whatever historical reasons—to be organized in such a
> way as to guarantee that a significant proportion of actors
> will not be able to perform their tasks as expected. (Grae-
> ber 2015, 71)

Graeber goes on to call this an example of utopian thinking. Bureaucracy is based on utopian thinking because it assumes people
to be perfect from its own point of view. Dirty data are simply real
data in the sense of documenting the struggle of real people with
a bureaucracy that exploits for its own ends the reality of unevenly
implemented digital technology with all its real-life defects. Grae-
bers mother died before she was accepted into the Medicaid program. The endless labor of filling completely meaningless forms is
a new form of domestic labor in the sense that it is not considered
labor at all and assumed to be provided "voluntarily" or performed
by underpaid so-called data janitors. Yet all the seemingly swift and
invisible action of algorithms, their elegant optimization of everything, their recognition of patterns and anomalies, are based on
the endless and utterly senseless labor of providing the required or
even utterly useless data.

Dirty data thus become, so to speak, a remainder of reality in
systems that are pegged to ideal models, averages, and Platonic
assumptions, inspired by an ideal fictional world in which brown
teens are poor by default, doctors just love to cooperate with
attempts to get rid of them entirely and people trying to claim

[Figure 1.1.] 33rd square. Google's Deep Dream Generator. [Screenshot, 2015, available at http://www.33rdsquare.com/2015/06/googles-inceptionism-lets-us-look-at.html, Accessed March 31, 2018.]

benefits are anomalies by definition and get treated (or are left untreated) accordingly. Sometimes "dirty data" record the passive resistance against permanent extraction of unacknowledged labor. This "signal" however is partly already determined by probability and preexisting models.

Corporate Animism

A brilliant example for apophenic pattern recognition was recently provided by a Google development team.[7] The point is that in order to "recognize" anything, neural networks need first to be taught what to recognize. Then, in a quite predictable loop they end up "recognizing" the things they were taught.

In Google's brilliant experiment, image recognition filters were looped on sheer random noise. There was nothing to recognize

since nothing was represented or even hidden in the noise. But
the shapes that started emerging were combinations of the shapes
and animals the networks had been taught to "see" earlier on. They
ended up "over-recognizing" these shapes, so to speak.

This process reveals the presets of computer vision, its hardwired ideologies and preferences. The result: a rainbow-colored
mess of disembodied fractal eyes, mostly without lids, inces-
santly surveilling their audience in a strident display of pattern
over-identification.

Google calls the act of creating pattern or image from noise
"inceptionism." It also calls this mode of image production "deep
dreaming." But in a very materialist sense, these entities are far
from hallucinations. If they are dreams, those dreams can be
interpreted as condensations or displacements of the current
technological disposition. They reveal how signal and noise are
defined by preexisting categories and probability. If you had
trained a neural network to "recognize" Hegel's master and slaves,
you might have ended up with sheer noise miraculously transform-
ing into Instagrams of an Art Basel Miami VIP preview staffed with
temp catering workers.

In a feat of unexpected genius, inceptionism manages to visualize
the unconscious of prosumer networks:[8] images surveilling users,
constantly registering their eye movements, behavior, and preferences, in aesthetic terms helplessly adrift between a knockoff of a
Hundertwasser coffee mug and an Art Deco frieze gone ballistic.
They show not so much the so-called Five Eyes of state surveillance
but the Eyes Unlimited of corporate surveillance, state surveillance,
deep state surveillance, academic ranking scores, likability metrics,
and so on and so on: Walter Benjamin's "optical unconscious"
updated to the unconscious of computational image production
(Benjamin 1974).

By "recognizing" things that were "not given," inceptionist neural
networks eventually end up effectively identifying a new totality

of aesthetic and social relations. They visualize the filters of computational vision. Presets are applied, regardless whether they "apply" or not: "The results are intriguing—even a relatively simple neural network can be used to over-interpret an image, just like as children we enjoyed watching clouds and interpreting the random shapes" (Mordvintsev, Olah, and Tyka 2015).

Inceptionist image production is decisively different from previous chemical or even electronic photographic procedures, posing new questions concerning realism and veracity. If previous techniques relied on myths of mechanical or optical "objectivity" and ultimately on optics and geometry, in the case of inceptionist image production vision appears to rely on pattern recognition, based on implanting pseudo-platonic forms into sensing technology and running the lot on petabytes of spam. The verisimilitude of vision is not based on assumptions about objective hardware but on the replication of brain functions (or what are currently believed to be brain functions). But in terms of veracity, this is a terrible choice indeed; no one really thinks that human brains make good witnesses. They project, speculate, invent, embellish, forget, and extrapolate. They also see faces in clouds, sometimes. As a consequence, cameras based on brain functions provide dubious testimony. Reproduction of reality becomes a matter of likelihood. Likeness collapses into probability.

But inceptionism is not just a digital hallucination. It is a document of an era that trains its smart phones to identify kittens, thus hardwiring truly terrifying jargons of cutesy into its means of prosumption. It demonstrates a version of corporate animism in which commodities are not only fetishes but dreamed-up, franchised chimeras. Yet these are deeply realist representations. According to Györgi Lukács, "classical realism" creates "typical characters" as they represent the objective social (and in this case technological) forces of our times (Idris 2005). Thus, inceptionism unlocks the black box of image recognition to release an almost medieval zoo of phantasmagoric creatures locked inside.

[Figure 1.2.] A plate of spaghetti meatballs returning our gaze. [Image: Thorne Brandt, available at: https://twitter.com/thornebrandt/status/617173618238332928?lang=en, accessed August 1, 2018.]

Inceptionism gives those forces a face—or more precisely unlimited eyes. The creature that stares at you from your plate of meatballs is not an amphibian beagle, though. It is the ubiquitous surveillance of networked image production, a type of memetically modified intelligence that watches you in the form of the lunch that you will Instagram in a second if it doesn't attack you first.

Imagine a world of enslaved objects remorsefully scrutinizing you. Your car, your yacht, your art collection is watching you with a gloomy and utterly depressed expression. You may own us, they seem to say, but we're going to inform on you. You will start missing Althusser's lonely police officer, because now you are being interpellated 24/7 by a serving of dog pasta. And then just guess as to what kind of creature we'll re-cognize in you!

This question of recognition recalls and reveals the enduring power of the Turing test as a mode of identification and reveals the segregation at the core of assessing machine learning. Turing's

[Figure 1.3.] The shape in this flock of birds over New York appears to be the face of President Vladimir Putin. [Screenshot of video by Sheryl Gilbert, available at: https://www.youtube.com/watch?v=h-7-Ej_Nulg, accessed August 1, 2018.]

game was successful if a machine had the same ability as a human to confuse an interrogator about its gender. But contemporary computation is not about confusion of identity but multiplication of identities. Facebook, for example, has modified the imitation game to say: if you don't want to identify as man or as woman that's fine, but please check one of these fifty-plus boxes to state your precisely defined other type of gender, and we'll make sure to send you the appropriate adds. This is not an imitation game but an identification game.

Similarity—or correlation—as mathematical evidence is something Turing discussed as well. To challenge his own ideas, he cited the objection that machines could never bond over strawberries and cream like humans. But he answered his own challenge with a complex twist: Yes, a machine cannot bond with a man in the same way that a white man will bond with a white man over strawberries with cream and a black man will bond with a black man over straw-

berries with cream. But—and this is my conclusion, not Turing's—if
a machine reproduced this behavior, would this machine then be
thinking?[9]

Some people think so. Because the idea of white guys bonding over
strawberries and cream has moved to the heart of social-network
analysis. This is a pristine example of so-called homophily, a concept further discussed by Wendy Chun (see Chun in this volume).
Homophily means that people like to bond with similar people.
How could this produce mathematical evidence of anything? If
white men mostly have strawberries and cream with white men,
this means that whoever a white man has strawberries with is most
likely a white man. This is what Facebook packages into the idea
that you are like what you like, and that you will like the things that
people who are like you like. This is how they sell you strawberries
with cream. And this is also how Google concludes you are not
a robot. You are not a robot because someone who likes similar
things checked the box to say he is not a robot and this applies
to you by correlation. If you extend this thinking to the imitation
game, you can guess not only the gender of all the players but all
their friends and their social network. This is how the game starts
transgressing its own boundaries and slowly becomes real.

So there are two completely different games at hand. On the one
hand, the identification game: if something looks like something,
it is the same. All boxes get checked. On the other hand, Turing's
imitation game: maybe something that looks similar is the same.
It's definitely possible that someone who comes across as a man is
a man. Then again maybe not. At this point, a thinking machine will
decide that this is not the interrogator's business. The best choice
is to politely move on to a protracted and paradoxical discussion of
the weather.

Apophenia

Inceptionism proves that pattern recognition also exists where
there is no pattern but a form is detected nevertheless. This

process is called *apophenia*.[10] A major example of this is to recognize creatures in clouds. Apophenia is defined as the perception of random patterns within random data. As Benjamin Bratton recently argued, apophenia is about "drawing connections and conclusions from sources with no direct connection other than their indissoluble perceptual simultaneity" (Bratton 2013).

Are the patterns "recognized" in the sea of data today just superstitious mumbo-jumbo? Is apophenia an updated form of divination? Photography was once famously described as soothsaying by Walter Benjamin: "[I]s not every corner of our cities a scene of action? Is not each passerby an actor? Is it not the task of the photographer—descendant of the augurs and the haruspices— to uncover guilt and name the guilty in his pictures?" (Benjamin 1974, 25).

Still, there is a crucial distinction between the twentieth-century photographer and the filterers and analysts of the twenty-first. The new pattern extractors are not mainly supposed to recognize the guilty after the fact. They are expected to predict the perpetrator as well as the crime before it has been able to occur. Every spot of our cities is mapped out as a probable crime site, fully decked with gender- and age-based targeted advertising, and surveilled by animated commodities, divinatory cellphone cameras, and aerial views from tapped drones.

The twenty-first-century augur creates the image before the event, anticipating its effect and calling forth reality. The arrow of time has reversed, but the flow of time is unstable and has become essentially unpredictable.

However apophenia also has a creative aspect.

Back in the Neolithic, humans imagined star constellations and observed patterns of movement by projecting animal shapes into the skies. Let's say they saw a crab and called this constellation Cancer. Even though there was no actual crab in space, constellations like

these served as working hypotheses to eventually come up with
fundamentally different worldviews.

One could laugh about the poor naïve people of the period who insisted on seeing nonexistent shapes in the skies. But by tenaciously sticking to projecting fictional figures into the cosmos, the fundamental movements of the solar system were uncovered. This didn't happen, though, because people believed crabs were walking in the cosmos; this happened because people came eventually to realize that there were (most probably) no crabs in the cosmos. Had they not they "seen" them though, they might have missed defining patterns in the movements of planets. But they would have also missed the patterns if they hadn't given up on the literal reality of the crabs.

But even more importantly all these activities also completely changed the organization of society. The analysis of planetary and star movements enabled the development of the calendar and agriculture. Cue irrigation, storage, breeding, architecture, sedentary lifestyles, and so on. Storage created the idea of property. Bands of hunters and gatherers were replaced by proto-states of farmer-kings and slaveholders, by vertical social hierarchies. Apophenia—as a part of magical thinking—contributed to all these transformations.

But what are we going to make of contemporary acts of apophenia? Are we to assume that computer vision has entered its own Neolithic phase of magical thinking and pattern projection? But if this is the case, one thing is very different. To keep expressing this through the example of crabs in space: computer vision still seems to be in the phase where it thinks that there really are crabs in space and that the patterns emerging from the cosmos of data are actually reality. Software engineers like saying about computers: garbage in, garbage out. In divinationist computer vision let's rephrase this as: crab in, crap out. Let's see faeces in clouds, while we are at it!

It might be more accurate though to assume that humanity has entered a second Neolithic, a phase of the reinvention of the technologies invented during this period. Today a lot of data-related vocabulary refers back to techniques first developed during the Neolithic. Data farming and harvesting, mining, and extraction point back to agricultural and metallurgic procedures. Today, expressions of life as reflected in data trails become a farmable, harvestable, minable resource managed by informational biopolitics. The stones and ores of the Neolithic are replaced by coltane, silicone, and Minecraft Red Stone. So what is the function of apophenia now, when new procedures of pattern "recognition" threaten to create new types of kings and slaveholders?[11]

Outside

Let's think back to the beginning and Althusser's policeman yelling, "Hey you!" In fact this really did happen to a person called George Michael, when he was apprehended in a Beverly Hills toilet after a plainclothes policeman had encouraged him to commit what U.S. legal jargon calls a "lewd" act. Michael was hailed, apprehended, and jailed. He had incorrectly recognized the pattern, or rather he had been duped into believing he was being chatted up. As a result LAPD went all "Hey you!" on poor George.

Arguably Michael has misinterpreted a pattern: he mistook a policeman yelling "Hey you" for a lover, an act of apophenia if there ever was one. And predictably, scorn and ridicule poured over him.

But, instead of apologizing or admitting an error of judgment, Michael brilliantly insisted on his perspective. He released a video called "Outside" in which this scene is retold and roles are flipped over; the men's lavatory turns into a dance floor, disco balls pop from the ceiling and squadrons of gay biker cops dance with one another. After all who said one needs to accept the LAPD's idea of a proper subjected subject? Michael insisted on recognizing patterns differently: "Hey you!" is not only an act of subjection but perhaps the most basic act of human communication, an act of acknowledgment and contact, perhaps even seduction. "Outside" was not only a coming out, not only a claiming of public space, but also an act of defiant apophenia.

This type of apophenia can cause serendipitous misreadings or end you up in jail, that is, but at least not as a docile subjected subject. It (mis-)reads the letter of the law for a love letter, it insists on not recognizing the other at all but rather knowing them in the biblical sense, not as sea of data but as flow of energy, not as pattern-of-life but as wave of desire. Who got the point—the tons of morons who laughed about George for not "getting it right," or George, who got it left so to speak and just cruised ahead of the pattern?

This is why I suggest we follow him and go outside, right now. Let's go.[12]

Coming in

But, wait. Where is outside? This question is less simple than it seems. And it may well turn out we don't have to go anywhere at all because we are outside already. At least the NSA thinks so. Didn't their writer complain about the "sea of data—data, data everywhere, but not one drop of information?"

Isn't this "sea of data" a big outside, in the most romantic and sublime sense of the word? An "unknown unknown" in Donald Rumsfeld's inimitable definition? Doesn't it look like the "big outdoors" heroically tackled by speculative realists? At the very least this wild and life-threatening sea of data is certainly not "the sofa" George Michael emphatically declares he's done with.

To give a bit less romantic examples: in terms of political geography the outside is increasingly difficult to pin down. More and more spaces are converted into extraterritorial enclaves and duty-free gated communities, into para-statelets and anti-"terrorist" operation zones, offshore entities and corporate proxy concessions, a configuration for which Keller Easterling brilliantly coined the term ExtraStateCraft (Easterling 2014). These areas are not—and this is crucial—outside of the system of nation-states but within, in-between, and in certain cases also over and underneath. We see this happening when—as in Lebanon or Italy—the idea of garbage in, garbage out no longer works. Instead it's garbage in, garbage in-between, garbage all over, and more to come. It's garbage inside out.

But if many of us are outside in already, either as dirty or clean data, as signal or noise, Graeber or Grueber; isn't a "coming out" at the same time a "coming in"?

Actually this is exactly how George Michael continues his argument. The "outside" is not about the romantic great outdoors of icebergs and posthuman reason, not about calculating being nor divining online shopping craves, nor terrorist threats from petabytes of garbage. "Outside" means: *servicing the community of flesh and bone* (nothing more).[13]

He sings:

> And yes, I've been bad
> Doctor, won't you do with me what you can
> You see I think about it all the time
> I'd service the community
> (but I already have you see!)
> I never really said it before
> There's nothing here but flesh and bone
> There's nothing more, nothing more
> There's nothing more
> Let's go outside

Mr. Michael counterinterpellates the policeman by challenging him to service the community. His version of a policeman does exactly that. But this community is no longer the same either. It is not a world where people end up as dirty data and dead brown teenagers, stuck with overflowing garbage in the paradoxical no-man's-lands of statistical bureaucracy and overall exception.

Rather this needs to be a world in which everything looks just the same, just seen from a completely different angle. How does this work? Imagine someone who was sent out into space to investigate whether the pattern that was detected in the endlessly vast data set of the cosmos is actually there. In the Neolithic this was impossible but not now. Let's say the predicted pattern is: alien intelligence exists, it is evil and everywhere, and in order to create patterns to contain it, we need to compute all the data in the universe. The person then ventures out into the vast ocean of spam and penis enlargement ads to look for this mythical creature. But then the person has a brilliant idea. She asks herself: How about accepting that the projection may or may not correspond to reality? Intelligent evil aliens may exist or not, just as crabs, lions, and scorpions too might actually exist somewhere in the depths of the cosmos. We cannot exclude it. Maybe we could even calculate it if we just keep crunching numbers. But how about this question: Do intelligent humans exist at all? This person might then discover potential samples of this species inside the spacecraft's own toilet.

It turns out that the intelligent person in the toilet is George Michael. And then she realizes that her space travel is not extra-terrestrial at all but intraterrestrial. The ExtraSpaceCraft she's been flying never left the launchpad as funding for space missions got cut. The cosmos she saw was some sort of projection of U.S. health insurance data. Infuriated, she asks George Michael to immediately reform police services. He politely points out that policing can be seen from a different angle as well: as servicing the community of those who keep on being crunched as overpoliced dirty data, or ignored as underpoliced inhabitants of all sort of failed states, platinum card lounges, and other examples of extraterritorial contemporary geographies. Seen from the latter perspective, just condemning policing is not going to make things better. Both blatant over- and underpolicing combine into the destruction of the common.

Let's leave the detailed description of the different modes of servicing the community of flesh and bone to Mr. Michael. But from this perspective the sea of data turns out to be the mess of human relations (nothing more). Althusser's model of recognition and policing suggests that you need to sacrifice the common like a haruspex slaughters a sacrificial animal. Next you filter faeces from its intestines to predict and master future risk and thus create new empires of data barons and stakeholders. It's a bit rough, frankly.

In contrast one could first of all accept that what is portrayed as an external and threatening sea of data that needs to be sifted, filtered, cleansed, and purified is basically the mess of human nature. One might as well have fun with it.

This is not to say that this will be any more rational. It will not be more beautiful, noble, or true either. There will be plenty of crabs and crap to deal with, not to mention evil humans and intelligent aliens. Just ask yourself: do you prefer to dance in an ExtraSpace-Craft toilet? Or would you rather fill out forms all day?

Notes

1   "Conspiracy . . . is the poor person's cognitive mapping in the postmodern age; it is a degraded figure of the total logic of late capital, a desperate attempt to represent the latter's system, whose failure is marked by its slippage into sheer theme and content" (Jameson 1988, 356).

2   I use the word *paranoia* here to refer to its usage in cultural theory rather than in its psychopathological definition. For a different approach, focusing more on the symptoms of paranoia (of which apophenia is only one, albeit a very important one), see Apprich in this volume.

3   "The world of finance capital is that perpetual present—but it is not a continuity; it is a series of singularity-events" (Jameson 2015, 122).

4   The NSA was spying on World of Warcraft. Seriously.

5   Spambots are also seen as an example of possible distortion of big-data veracity.

6   "In late June and early July 1991, twelve million people across the country (mostly Baltimore, Washington, Pittsburgh, San Francisco, and Los Angeles) lost phone service due to a typographical error in the software that controls signals regulating telephone traffic. One employee typed a '6' instead of a 'D.' The phone companies essentially lost all control of their networks."

7   My thanks to Ben Bratton for pointing out this fact and to Linda Stupart for mentioning apophenia as a term used by William Gibson.

8   A prosumer is a mix between a producer and a consumer, a consuming producer or the other way round.

9   He clearly states: "The works and customs of mankind do not seem to be very suitable material to which to apply scientific induction. A very large part of

space-time must be investigated, if reliable results are to be obtained. Otherwise we may (as most English children do) decide that everybody speaks English, and that it is silly to learn French" (Turing 1950, 448).

10   Thank you to Linda Stupart for drawing my attention to this notion. For further discussion of the concept of apophenia in the context of paranoia, see Apprich in this volume.

11   Apophenia is a misextraction, an act of failing interpellation and recognition that can have social consequences. As several people pointed out, data can also be misunderstood as Dada. Ways of collaging data have characterized current popular aesthetics. The creation of improbable combinations and the crossing of the limits of the likely can be interpreted as a silent and even involuntary act of rebellion against pattern recognition. The manufacturing of improbable and implausible objects via all sorts of data manipulation tools is a way of confusing automated ways of recognition—face recognition, recognition of behavioral patterns, recognition of shapes, and the simultaneous creation of categories of political recognition.

12   I wrote this when George Michael was still alive, and I miss him dearly.

13   Thank you to Brian Kuan Wood for pointing this out.

References

Althusser, Louis. 1971. "On Ideology and Ideological State Apparatuses: Notes Towards an Investigation." In *Lenin and Philosophy and Other Essays*, 121–73. London: New Left Books.

Benjamin, Walter. 1974. "A Short History of Photography," trans. Stanley Mitchell, *Screen* 13 (1): 5-26.

Bratton, Benjamin. 2013. "Some Traces of Effects of the Post-Anthropocene: On Accelerationist Geopolitical Aesthetics." *e-flux Journal* 46. Accessed July 20, 2015. http://www.e-flux.com/journal/some-trace-effects-of-the-post-anthropocene-on -accelerationist-geopolitical-aesthetics/.

Cabrera, Amanda. 2015. "A Halloween Special: Tales from the Dirty Data Crypt." *Datamentors*. Accessed October 30, 2015. http://www.datamentors.com/blog/ halloween-special-tales-dirty-data-crypt.

Easterling, Keller. 2014. *Extrastatecraft: The Power of Infrastructural Space*. London: Verso.

Graeber, David. 2015. *The Utopia of Rules: On Technology, Stupidity, and the Secret Joys of Bureaucracy*. Brooklyn, N.Y.: Melville House.

Idris, Farhad B. 2005. "Realism." In *Encyclopedia of Literature and Politics: Censorship, Revolution, and Writing,* Volume 3: *H–R,* ed. M. Keith Booker, 601. Westport, Conn.: Greenwood.

Jameson, Fredric. 1988. "Cognitive Mapping." In *Marxism and the Interpretation of Culture,* ed. Cary Nelson and Lawrence Grossberg, 347–60. Champaign: University of Illinois Press.

Jameson, Fredric. 2009. *The Geopolitical Aesthetic*. Indianapolis: Indiana University Press.

22   Jameson, Fredric. 2015. "The Aesthetics of Singularity." *New Left Review* 92:101–32.

Kopytoff, Verne. 2014. "Big Data's Dirty Problem." *Fortune.* Accessed June 30, 2014. http://fortune.com/2014/06/30/big-data-dirty-problem/.

Lohr, Steven. 2014. "For Big-Data Scientists, 'Janitor Work' Is Key Hurdle to Insights." *New York Times.* Accessed August 17, 2014. http://www.nytimes.com/2014/08/18/technology/for-big-data-scientists-hurdle-to-insights-is-janitor-work.html?_r=0.

Mordvintsev, Alexander, Christopher Olah, and Mike Tyka. 2015. "Inceptionism: Going Deeper into Neural Networks." *Google Research Blog.* Accessed May 13, 2017. https://ai.googleblog.com/2015/06/inceptionism-going-deeper-into-neural.html.

Normandeau, Kevin. 2013. "Beyond Volume, Variety, and Velocity Is the Issue of Big Data Veracity." *Inside Big Data.* Accessed September 30, 2013. http://insidebigdata.com/2013/09/12/beyond-volume-variety-velocity-issue-big-data-veracity/.

Russon, Mary-Ann. 2015. "Google DeepDream Robot: 10 Weirdest Images Produced by AI 'Inceptionism' and Users Online." *International Business Times.* Accessed July 6, 2015. http://www.ibtimes.co.uk/google-deepdream-robot-10-weirdest-images-produced-by-ai-inceptionism-users-online-1509518.

Sontheimer, Michael. 2015. "Interview with Julian Assange." *Spiegel.* Accessed July 20, 2015. http://www.spiegel.de/international/world/spiegel-interview-with-wikileaks-head-julian-assange-a-1044399.html.

Sprenger, Florian. 2015. *The Politics of Micro-Decision: Edward Snowden, Net Neutrality, and the Architectures of the Internet.* Lüneburg: meson press.

Steyerl, Hito. 2014. "Proxy Politics: Signal and Noise." *e-flux Journal* 60. Accessed December, 2014. http://www.e-flux.com/journal/60/61045/proxy-politics-signal-and-noise/.

Turing, Alan M. 1950. "Computing Machinery and Intelligence." Mind. A Quarterly Review of Psychology and Philosophy 59 (236): 433-460.

Wikipedia, the free encyclopedia. 2017a. "Data Mining." *Wikipedia.* Accessed January 17, 2017. https://en.wikipedia.org/wiki/Data_mining.

Wikipedia, the free encyclopedia. 2017b. "Pareidolia." *Wikipedia.* Accessed January 17, 2017. https://en.wikipedia.org/wiki/Pareidolia.

2

Crapularity Hermeneutics: Interpretation as the Blind Spot of Analytics, Artificial Intelligence, and Other Algorithmic Producers of the Postapocalyptic Present

Florian Cramer

Hermeneutics and Analytics

"Language is easy to capture but difficult to read," in the words of the poet and media researcher John Cayley (Cayley 2012). Cayley wrote this sentence merely as a footnote to an essay on his "terms of reference," yet it sums up the whole dilemma of so-called Big Data processing. Data "analytics" deals with the same structural problem that the oracle priests of Delphi tried to solve: how to make sense out of an endless stream of (drug-induced) gibberish? Or, as Hito Steyerl noted in the previous chapter—how to transform the *garbled noise* of *women, children, slaves, and foreigners* into the proper speech of *male locals . . . labeled citizens*? Even when one ignores the politics involved, the questions still remain: To what degree will the method of interpretation influence the outcome? Who gets to choose the method? Which real-world consequences will the interpretation have?

Delphi became one of the birthplaces of hermeneutics, the theological-philological discipline of exegesis: without expert interpretation, first through priests, later through philologists, gibberish would have remained gibberish. Literary studies secularized hermeneutics in the nineteenth century, and Freud's psychoanalysis—the close reading of the gibberish captured from a patient's subconscious—made it medical and thus applied science. Intelligence agencies, investment banks, and internet companies turned analysis into analytics.[1] In order to quickly make sense of captured data, computer analytics had to take shortcuts in the process from capturing to reading, by jumping from syntax to pragmatics, by operationalizing and thus simplifying semantic interpretation in the process.

Computational analytics—whether performed by intelligence services, on stock markets, or on web server logs—is limited to what can be expressed as quantitative-syntactical operations to be performed by algorithms. This conversely changes the perspective on the gibberish. Rather than a narrative in need of exegesis, it is now a data set in need of statistics. As Johanna Drucker pointed out,

> the abandonment of interpretation in favor of a naïve approach to statistical [analysis] certainly skews the game from the outset in favor of a belief that data is intrinsically quantitative—self-evident, value neutral, and observer-independent. This belief excludes the possibilities of conceiving data as qualitative, co-dependently constituted. (Drucker 2011)

Yet it could be argued that data is always qualitative, even when its processing is quantitative: this is why algorithms and analytics dis-

criminate, in the literal as well as in the broader sense of the word,
whenever they recognize patterns (see Foreword to this volume).

The Politics of Scores

A staple part of Fluxus festivals in the 1960s were Emmett Williams's *Counting Songs* (1962), which consisted of the artists on stage counting the audience members one by one. Aside from being early pieces of performance art and poetry, minimal music and concept art, they also served the pragmatic purpose of obtaining "an exact head count to make sure that the management [of the festival venues] wasn't cheating us" (Williams 1991, 32). With the same shortcut from instruction to pragmatics as in today's computer analytics, Williams's score was thus a simple data-mining algorithm. The semantic interpretation of the piece was left to the audience, which in the 1960s was likely to have read the piece as absurd theater in the tradition of Ionesco and Beckett rather than as a musical-poetic performance in the tradition of John Cage's and La Monte Young's event scores. Today's audiences might be inclined to associate the *Counting Songs* with the counting of individuals in other confined spaces such as kindergartens, aircrafts, and refugee camps. Like other Fluxus pieces, the *Counting Songs* have been commonly read as participatory artworks, since they cannot exist by themselves but instead are structurally dependent on their audience. Yet they effectively establish and reinforce the various divides between the artist-composer, the performers who execute the score instructions, and the audience upon whom the score is performed. As data processing, the piece thus contains the hierarchy of programmer, program, and data while selling the same illusion of participation and interaction with which "interactive systems," from computer games to social networking platforms, are being sold today. With their instruction code and performance, however, the *Counting Songs* openly expose this manipulation, like a Brechtian theater of algorithm. (The Fluxus artist who most consequently worked in the medium of minimalist instruction scores coincidentally adopted the name George Brecht. Born George MacDiarmid, he had previously worked as a chemist conducting research and development on tampons at Johnson & Johnson.)

On the level of their pragmatics, the *Counting Songs* may be interpreted as an early piece of crisis computing.[2] Williams recalls that

> sometimes, there were more performers than spectators at these "public performances." And sometimes, when the audience outnumbered the performers, the spectators took advantage of the situation. One night, students climbed up onto the stage, harried the performers, and tried to set fire to the score of my *Opera.* And once, during a performance, in Amsterdam, a girl tried to set Dick Higgins on fire. (1991, 32)

The suspicion that managers tried to cheat the artists proved true, since "our share of the gate on the first night of the festival had been considerably smaller than the standing-room-only crowd had led us to expect" (32). As crisis computing, the *Counting Songs* thus enact the notion of "crisis" in its original Greek meaning (decision) as well as in its contemporary sense (state of exception). The songs perform decision-making through computing, with the purpose of regaining control in a state of exception. However, an inherent issue of the *Counting Songs* is their necessity, as a fixed data-mining algorithm for computational analytics, to always anticipate the state of exception. They could only react to a crisis scenario that the Fluxus artists were already familiar with and that predictably repeated itself at each new festival location. But how can a state of exception live up to its name when it has become predictable? How would the *Counting Songs* deal, for example, with an overnight *Brexit* in which the Fluxus artists would lose their permit to commercially perform as foreigners? How would the *Songs* deal with a sudden monetary crash that invalidates all cash, leaving people only with the possibility to pay for online services through crypto-

currencies? How would they deal with nonpaying refugees seeking
shelter in a festival venue?

The reduction of audience members to countable numbers—
data sets, indices—is thus a self-fulfilling prophecy of stability. Its
production of numbers would remain perfectly self-referential,
even if the counting instructions were riddled with bugs or were
combined with instructions from others scores (such as, for example, Takehisa Kosugi's *Music for a Revolution,* which requires the
performer to "Scoop out one of your eyes 5 years from now and
do the same with the other eye 5 years later" [Sohm, Szeemann,
and Kölnischer Kunstverein 1970]) in such a way that would result
in interferences and unpredictable system behavior. Today, such
complexity nightmares have become everyday phenomena, from
computer crashes to Y2K bugs, and in popular fiction such as the
Robocop character (in Paul Verhoeven's original 1987 film), whose
circuits simply shut down when his programmed instructions—to
arrest criminals—conflict with another programmed instruction
to never arrest board members of Omni Consumer Products, the
company that constructed him and that runs Detroit's privatized
city administration and police force.

Common wisdom in crisis computing is to increase the complexity
of algorithms so that systems can cope with the complex realities
they encounter. The instruction set for Williams's *Counting Songs*
could be extended to also include behavioral rules for Brexit and
other states of exception, or to cope with a fascist regime under
which counting people has become the privilege of private warfare
contractors. What becomes of performance art, with its implicit
program of disrupting static social situations, when it has to operate in situations of maximum social disruption? How could a Fluxus
score be performed in a territory overwhelmed by drone warfare
or controlled by gangland criminality?

The popular narratives for these scenarios are, of course, not to be
found in Fluxus. From 2005 to 2010, CBS television broadcast the

series *NUMB3RS* with plots revolving around modern mathematics being applied to solve crimes (Scott and Scott 2005–2010). The show's two main characters were an FBI agent and his brother, a professor of applied mathematics who becomes drawn toward police work through his tireless invention of algorithms that predict behavioral patterns of crime suspects and the probability of future crime scenes. When the show first aired, the term "Big Data" had not yet been coined. There were, however, historical precursors to algorithmic law enforcement. When the bombings and kidnappings of the extreme-left Baader-Meinhof group reached a climax in West Germany in 1977, Federal Criminal Police director Horst Herold ran population databases through mainframe computers in order to narrow down the list of terrorist suspects. The Hamburg-based punk band Abwärts ("Downward") reacted to this in 1980 with their song "Computerstaat" ("Computer State"). It sketches a paranoid-apocalyptic present in which Arafat and Brezhnev turn up and hang out in the homes of good West German citizens, with the KGB invading their forests and sewers, and World War III breaking out on their vacation spots. The refrain of the song is:

> Germany catastrophe state
> We live in the computer state
> We live in the computer state
> We live in the computer state.[3]

The LP on which the song was released ends with a sound sample of Horst Herold warning Baader-Meinhof members that they would eventually crack under the pressure of the police manhunt against them. The final statement of his speech, "wir kriegen sie alle"— "we'll get them all"—is pressed into an endlessly repeating lock groove on the record. This way, the analog audio medium emulates the cybernetic feedback loop of a computerized dragnet search.

Not much seems to have changed between 1977 and 2017 in the use of technology and the state of world affairs, if one replaces Arafat with the Islamic State of Iraq and Syria (ISIS), Brezhnev with Putin, the KGB with the FSB and perhaps Stalingrad with 9/11. Pre-

dictive policing had already been imagined much earlier, notably
in Philip K. Dick's 1956 short story *Minority Report*. The story's film
adaption by Steven Spielberg in 2002 featured three-dimensional
computer interfaces, which likely paved the way for the visual
aesthetics and mainstream television success of *NUMB3RS* in 2005.
On the surface, *NUMB3RS* might have seemed no more than an updated version of the 1950s radio and television show *Dragnet*; the
police method featured in *Dragnet,* of searching criminals by gradually narrowing down lists of suspects, was itself updated/renewed
in real life in 1970s Germany using mainframe computers for
dragnet searches, a method strongly proposed and advocated
by Horst Herold and reflected in Abwärts' song *Computerstaat*. In
Minority Report, predictive policing was pure science fiction with no
basis in real technology. But *NUMB3RS* for the first time presented
modern computer-based analytics in each of its episodes. The
formulas, statistics, and algorithms in *NUMB3RS* were neither old-
school database searches, nor Hollywood smoke-and-mirrors, but
genuine mathematics and fairly realistic cases of modern "Big Data"
analytics. Wolfram Research, the developers of the Mathematica
software package and the Wolfram Alpha search engine, were
employed as the show's scientific consultants to make sure that
all the mathematics presented in the episodes were real and that
the algorithms and visualization could work. The producers of the
series were the brothers Ridley and Tony Scott, whose feature films
Black Hawk Down (2001) and *Top Gun* (1985) were about modern
warfare and had been produced with direct support from the U.S.
Army (and in the case of *Top Gun,* also with financial support from
the U.S. Department of Defense); conversely, Tony Scott's 1998 film
Enemy of the State presented a dystopic, technologically realistic
scenario of NSA communication surveillance.

Whether or not *NUMB3RS* should be read as an early 2000s
military-industrial sales pitch for 2010s Big Data and predictive policing technology, the analytics of each episode lends itself perfectly
to critical review by civil rights activists as well as digital humanities
scholars. Today, it is a widely reported fact that data sets and

algorithms, or the combination of both, can and do discriminate. In 2016, an op-ed piece in the *New York Times* called for the need to "Make Algorithms Accountable" in relation to algorithmically computed "risk scores" for creditors and prospective criminals (Angwin 2016). In an article for the same newspaper, Kate Crawford, a professor at NYU and founder of the AI Institute, referred to this as "A.I.'s [= artificial intelligence's] White Guy Problem":

> Sexism, racism and other forms of discrimination are being built into the machine-learning algorithms that underlie the technology behind many "intelligent" systems that shape how we are categorized and advertised to.
>
> Take a small example from last year: Users discovered that Google's photo app, which applies automatic labels to pictures in digital photo albums, was classifying images of black people as gorillas. Google apologized; it was unintentional.
>
> But similar errors have emerged in Nikon's camera software, which misread images of Asian people as blinking, and in HewlettPackard's web camera software, which had difficulty recognizing people with dark skin tones. (Crawford 2016)

Crawford also mentions predictive policing as problematic, since "software analyses of large sets of historical crime data are used to forecast where crime hot spots are most likely to emerge," thus "perpetuating an already vicious cycle" with "more surveillance in traditionally poorer, nonwhite neighborhoods, while wealthy, whiter neighborhoods are scrutinized even less."[4]

When in 2005 the pilot episode of *NUMB3RS* featured crime hotspot mapping through mathematical formulas implemented into computer algorithms, this was presented as the convergence of police work and clean-room lab science. The reality of the technology, however, is not quite as spotless. In 2016, the American nonprofit investigative journalism platform ProPublica found that "there's software used across the country to predict future criminals.

And it's biased against blacks" (Angwin et al. 2016). Surveying the algorithmically computed "risk scores" of more than 7,000 people arrested in Broward County, Florida, in 2013 and 2014, ProPublica concluded that the "score proved remarkably unreliable in forecasting violent crime: Only 20 percent of the people predicted to commit violent crimes actually went on to do so." The algorithm "was particularly likely to falsely flag black defendants as future criminals, wrongly labeling them this way at almost twice the rate as white defendants. . . . White defendants were mislabeled as low risk more often than black defendants" (Angwin et al. 2016). Furthermore, the algorithm that assessed the risk score was not developed by the police or by any other government agency, nor was it published; rather, it was developed and kept as a trade secret by the private company Northpointe (a subsidiary of the Canadian Volaris Group), whose stated mission is "to improve correctional decision making at the level of individual offender case decisions, and at the level of system-wide policy, planning, and program evaluation" (Northpointe 2016).

In practice, predictive policing programs extend to a principle of tightly policing neighborhoods identified through analytics as crime hotspots. In 2014, a spokesperson for the American Civil Liberties Union called this principle "guilt by association": "Because you live in a certain neighborhood or hang out with certain people, we are now going to be suspicious of you and treat you differently, not because you have committed a crime or because we have information that allows us to arrest you, but because our predictive tool shows us you might commit a crime at some point in the future" (Eligon and Williams 2015).

Positivism Dispute Redux

The *MIT Technology Review,* a periodical whose overall perspective on technology tends to be optimistic and trustful, published in 2016 an article on how artificial intelligence analytics "Reveals the Hidden Sexism of Language" (arXiv 2016). A neural network trained with mainstream news media articles as its data set would answer the question "father : doctor :: mother : x" with "x = nurse" and "man : computer programmer :: woman : x" with "x = homemaker." (arXiv 2016). The problem is not only in the semantic bias of the data set, but also in the design of the algorithm that treats the data as unbiased fact, and finally in the users of the computer program who believe in its scientific objectivity.

The issue of discrimination and even killings of people based on hidden biases in computing is nothing new. The 1982 book *The Network Revolution* by the computer scientist Jacques Vallee begins with the following account:

> On Friday, 9 November 1979, at 10 p.m., three young men driving on Highway 20 stopped at a gas station in Etampes, near Paris. . . . Mr. Nicolas, the service station operator, took a dim view of the tattered blue jeans, the leather jackets, the license number which did not look right because it was patched up with bits of black tape. . . . Nicolas . . . called the police to report the "suspicious" car and its even more disreputable occupants. In Etampes, police officers went to the computer terminal linking them with the central file of the Interior Ministry, in Paris, a file whose very existence had recently been denied by a Cabinet member. In response to a brief flurry of commands, the police entered the car's license number into the computer's memory for checking against its data bank. The system soon flashed its verdict: the vehicle was stolen. . . . A special night brigade was dispatched. The white and black police Renault intercepted the Peugeot driven by Francois at a red light. . . . The only police officer in uniform stayed inside the Renault: the other two, in civilian clothes, got out. One of them covered the Peugeot with his machine gun at the ready. The other stood in front of the suspect's car and armed his .357 Magnum. . . . A moment later, a shot rang out. The bullet went through the windshield and hit Claude's face just under the nose. . . .

Subsequent investigation disclosed that the car belonged
to Francois, who had bought it, legally, ten days before.
It had indeed been stolen in 1976, but it was soon recovered by the insurance company, which sold it to the
garage where Francois bought it. The computer file had
never been updated to reflect the change in the status of
the car. The central police records still regarded it as stolen property.[5] (Vallee 1982, 3–4)

Compared with 1970s and 1980s database dragnets, contemporary
Big Data analytics have only become more speculative, since their
focus is no longer on drawing conclusions for the present from the
past but on guessing the future, and since they no longer target
people based on the fact that their data matches other database
records but instead based on more speculative statistical proba-
bilities of environmental factors and behavioral patterns. Whether
or not human-created (and hence human-tainted) data is to be
blamed for discrimination, or for the hidden assumptions hard-
coded into algorithms that are employed for processing this data—
or whether machine-generated data can even be biased—they
all confirm Cayley's observation that language is "easy to capture
but difficult to read," that each operation of automated analytics
involves shortcuts from capturing to execution, from syntax to
pragmatics, leaving behind semantics and thorough critical interpretation as their collateral damage. This is as much illustrated by
the news story mentioned above as by each episode of *NUMB3Rs*,
which in forty-five minutes covers, besides a crime and its resolution, the finding of a mathematical model for a particular crime
and the translation of that model into an algorithm and computer
program (alongside such trivia as the brothers' conflicts with each
other and with their father, and one of the brother's relationship
with his grad student).

Critical discussions of data analytics, such as in the present
publication, inevitably reenact the positivism dispute of 1960s
continental European social sciences.[6] Its two main adversaries
were the Frankfurt School with its orientation toward hermeneutic

humanities, and Karl Popper, who argued in favor of a common methodological orientation of social and natural sciences towards problem solving (Popper 1962, 3). Popper, however, still distanced his position from pure quantitative science by insisting that "insight neither begins with perceptions or observations, nor with collection of data or facts, but it departs from *problems*"[7] (Popper 1962, 2). In light of this dispute, the twenty-first-century shift from interpretation towards analytics, and from problems towards data, amounts to a much more radical positivism than either Adorno or Popper imagined. Arguing against Popper and empirical sociology, Habermas stated in 1963 that

> the analytical-empirical modes of procedure tolerate only one type of experience which they themselves define. Only the controlled observation of physical behaviour, which is set up in an isolated field under reproducible conditions by subjects interchangeable at will, seems to permit intersubjectively valid judgments of perception. (Habermas 1976, 134)

From this perspective, the issues that Crawford and others observed in Big Data and artificial intelligence analytics are not limited to biases and skewed parameters *within* empirical "controlled observation"—for which the authors of the *MIT Technology Review* article propose, in all seriousness, a de-skewing algorithm (arXiv 2016). Rather, the bias lies in the *setup as such,* the "experience which they themselves define" (to again quote Habermas), which therefore involves a priori choices and decisions as well as unacknowledged biases. Interpretation hence constitutes the setup, while at the same time being disclaimed by the analysts. Hermeneutics, in other words, is always at work in analytics, though it is rarely acknowledged as such. The art theoretician Boris Groys identifies the internet corporations' business model of collecting their users' personal information—including "interests, desires, and needs"—as a "monetization of classical hermeneutics" in which "hermeneutic value" becomes a "surplus value" (Groys 2016, 179–80). Groys effectively blends the Frankfurt

School's 1940s critique of the culture industry with its 1960s critique of positivism, reflecting the early twenty-first-century status quo in which Silicon Valley has replaced Hollywood as the epitome of creative industries, with analytics of user-generated content rather than content production as its (multibillion dollar) business model.

Since an objective analytics, devoid of any interpretation and thus of any bias, does not exist, hermeneutics creeps in through the back door of analytics. This already begins at the point where data is captured, since almost any type of data acquisition requires subjective decision making (for example, concerning digital representation of color in scanned images).[8] Such technical-operational decisions become political when, for example, they concern accuracy of skin-tone reproduction, a problem that is not new but already existed in the days of analog film when filmmakers (including Jean-Luc Godard) boycotted Kodak due to the company's color and dynamic range calibration of film stocks, which was optimized for the reproduction of white skin and left black actors' faces underexposed.[9] In addition, data acquisition introduces its own artifacts—such as lens and microphone distortion, video and audio noise—whose retroactive filtering requires interpretative, often aesthetic decisions. Operators are interpreters. Though interpretation of data—or interpretation of sheet music by a musician—may be more confined than, for example, the interpretative reading of a novel, they are structurally no less hermeneutic.

From capturing to reading data, interpretation and hermeneutics thus creep into all levels of analytics. Biases and discrimination are only the extreme cases that make this mechanism most clearly visible. Interpretation thus becomes a bug, a perceived system failure, rather than a feature or virtue. As such, it exposes the fragility and vulnerabilities of data analytics. Analytics and hermeneutics thus relate to each other like the visible front end and the invisible back door in a piece of software, i.e. the kind of "backdoors" that remote attackers can exploit in order to gain control of a system. The "Hey you" with which the policeman talked George Michael into his "lewd" act (see Steyerl in this volume) embodies this duality: on the level of analytics, it is the primordial act of recognition and control described in the previous chapter. On the level of George Michael's hermeneutics, it was an erotic proposal; yet for the policeman, it was a disciplinary speech act that tactically encouraged erotic hermeneutics in order to be, in the end, all the more powerful as a disciplinary device.

Thus, hermeneutics becomes a backdoor practice in a libidinous sense. Not only does any network interface, as Chun pointed out, "act promiscuously" and does the internet leak by design (Chun 2016, 51), the fact that this promiscuity occurs on the level of technical automation (of network hardware as well as software) conversely obscures interpretative agency, including by intelligence and law enforcement agencies and intellectual property law firms that intercept and judicially interpret the network communications of surveilled individuals. Since this promiscuity does not happen on the front ends but on the back ends, through the backdoors and sometimes in the darkrooms of the internet, it is clandestine pro-miscuity and stigmatized hermeneutics; its practitioners will rarely come out of the closet the way Edward Snowden did. Historically, there may never have been as much interpretation going on as there is in the age of analytics, yet this paradoxically coincides with a blindness for the subjective viewpoints involved.

Drucker, too, insists on the crucial role of interpretation in the analysis (and visualization) of data, except that she is more optimis-tic regarding the necessity—rather than some backdoor repressed expression—of the humanities perspective. She argues that the

> natural world and its cultural corollary exist, but the humanistic concept of knowledge depends upon the interplay between a situated and circumstantial viewer and the objects or experiences under examination and interpretation. That is the basic definition of humanistic knowledge, and its graphical display must be specific to this definition in its very foundational principles. The challenge is enormous, but essential, if the humanistic

worldview, grounded in the recognition of the interpretative nature of knowledge, is to be part of the graphical expressions that come into play in the digital environment. (Drucker 2011)

The paradox of Big Data is that it both affirms and denies this "interpretative nature of knowledge." Just like the Oracle of Delphi, it is dependent on interpretation. But unlike the oracle priests, its interpretative capability is limited by algorithmics—so that the limitations of the tool (and, ultimately, of using mathematics to process meaning) end up defining the limits of interpretation. Similarly to Habermas, Drucker sees the danger of "ceding the territory of interpretation to the ruling authority of certainty established on the false claims of observer-independent objectivity" (Drucker 2011). This relates to her example of the visual perspective in which the graph of an epidemic is drawn, just as much as the interpretation of criminological data in alleged "hotspot" neighborhoods.

The territory of interpretation thus becomes a battleground between quantitative analytics and critical theory. In the latter, the mode of operation is always hermeneutic in the broad sense of being interpretative, discursive, and not privileging quantitative methodology, regardless of whether this methodology sails under hermeneutic, structuralist or materialist, humanist or posthumanist flags, and regardless of the debates between these schools. The question as to whether there is any qualitative difference between analytics and interpretation ultimately addresses the viability of artificial intelligence. If analytics can, hypothetically, render interpretation obsolete, then algorithms should ultimately be able to replace most sociologists, critics, and humanities scholars—or, at least, to render obsolete their hands-on interpretative work and shift their profession toward research and development of data analytics algorithms.

The Crapularity Is Here

Leaving aside all philosophical debates on artificial intelligence, current Big Data applications show that the viability of A.I. is not so much an epistemological issue but rather one of pure pragmatics. Whether or not A.I., or some types of A.I., are fundamentally flawed and unfit for their purpose, they nevertheless will be developed and used when they seem to get things done and when they deliver, most importantly, quantifiable results such as a decrease in crime statistics (no matter the social and political side effects), as well as cutting labor costs.

To put it in the words of one of A.I.'s most popular evangelists: *The Singularity Is Near* (Kurzweil 2005). But if the "singularity" is indeed near, this is not because machines or algorithms are becoming more intelligent (or just smarter, which is not the same thing). As shown in the previous chapter, "the markets" are the living proof that these machines or algorithms are no prerequisite for a "singularity" (see Steyerl in this volume). In this sense, the "singularity" has been around since at least the eighteenth century. According to Adam Smith's theory of the "invisible hand," the greed of individual economic actions does not matter since they neutralize each other's stupidity and thus together amount to an intelligent system.

The contemporary version of the "singularity" lacks such optimism because it will ultimately require society to dumb itself down. Machine utopias and dystopias would simply not be feasible otherwise, because the difficulties of making sense of information that is so easy to capture will still remain. As a countermeasure, culture and society must thus make themselves perfectly computer readable. When autonomous cars cause lethal highway accidents because their computer vision mistakes a white truck for a street sign—which is what happened to the A.I. autopilot of a Tesla car on May 7, 2016, in Williston, Florida—then this almost exactly fulfills the "Don't Drive Evil-ularity" scenario sketched in 2011 by the *Postnormal Times* researcher John A. Sweeney:

> Crash of Google-controlled robot car drives S&P to lower credit rating of USA, sending car loan rates and insurance premiums through the roof. Police suspect robot was watching Transcendent Man while driving. (Raford, Sweeney, and Pickard 2011)

In the case of crashed Tesla car, it was actually the human driver who was watching a Harry Potter movie (Levin and Woolf 2016). The long-term solution is not to improve the pattern recognition algorithms of cars, an endeavor as prone to overcomplexity and systemic failure as the extension of the Fluxus *Counting Songs* to crisis and catastrophe scenarios. Instead, all cars and highways could be redesigned and rebuilt in such a way as to make them failure-proof for computer vision and autopilots. For example, by painting all cars in the same specific colors, and with computer-readable barcode identifiers on all four sides, designing their bodies within tightly predefined shape parameters to eliminate the risk of confusion with other objects, by redesigning all road signs with QR codes and OCR-readable characters, by including built-in redundancies to eliminate misreading risks for computer vision systems, by straightening motorways to make them perfectly linear and moving cities to fit them, and by redesigning and rebuilding all cities to make them safe for inner-city autonomous car traffic.[10] In addition, all buildings—residences, offices, factories, hotels, stations, airports—could be redesigned so they can be fully serviced (cleaned, maintained, and front desk–clerked) by robots; a much more realistic scenario than speculating on breakthroughs in artificial intelligence systems such as computer vision and robotics that would, sometime in the future, make robots fit for servicing existing buildings. (This scenario has countless precursors in popular science fiction, including, for example, Stuart Gordon's 1996 movie *Space Truckers,* in which the protagonists transport square pigs that have been genetically modified to make more efficient use of limited spaceship cargo capacity. [Gordon 1997].)

Instead, "legacy" buildings that cannot be easily serviced by robots would likely become a surcharge luxury of the rich who can still afford human services. The singularity scenario would further entail, for example, a redesign of all education as automated online courses with computerized tests and certificates, leaving brick-and-mortar schools only for those who still can afford the higher tuition. The "social credit" system that China announced for its citizens in 2015, could become a worldwide model: each person's online activities receive positive or negative scores based on their supposed social productivity (in China: support of Communist Party politics), with access to—for instance—higher education and mortgage loans becoming dependent on a good credit score (Hatton 2015). Globally implemented, all automata that provide services or goods could accept "social credit" as payment so that this system could eventually replace traditional currencies. The "sharing economies" that are now provided by companies such as Uber and Airbnb could be scaled up to make them all-pervasive, allowing one to rent out all of one's belongings, even for the shortest periods of nonuse, as well as potential labor services. This would not so much be a means to generate surplus income but rather a socioecological austerity measure and necessity for everyone (except the rich) to make ends meet. Such systems could, after all, be introduced by liberal politicians as ostensible measures against nationalist, racist, and fascist backlashes in public opinion, promising liberal voters to fight prejudice and class or race privilege with a universal meritocracy based on objective (and thus fair) quantitative measurements.

The "singularity" described above could be achieved using today's technology. It would not even require any further fundamental research in the field of machine cognition, or any algorithms and chips that do not yet exist. Software and hardware research could even be stopped in order to yield the additional benefit of standardization based on a few optimized machine designs mass-produced at lower cost, which would conversely allow for a greater number of chips to be included in everyday devices.

In his contribution to a 2011 collaborative document on *Alternatives to the Singularity,* the technology anthropologist Justin Pickard characterized the corresponding present state of affairs as the "crapularity":

> 3D printing + spam + micropayments = tribbles that you get billed for, as it replicates wildly out of control. 90% of everything is rubbish, and it's all in your spare room—or someone else's spare room, which you're forced to rent through AirBnB. (Raford, Sweeney, and Pickard 2011)

The degree to which this dystopia has become our present-day reality can be monitored through the popular Twitter feed "Internet of Shit," which currently has 213,000 subscribers. ("Internet of Shit" 2015) Under the motto "The Internet of Shitty Things is here. Have all of your best home appliances ruined by putting the internet in them!" the microblog publishes—for example—Windows "blue screens of death" in elevators, ransomware messages on train station displays, and a car performing a software update on its central computer console while it is being driven (Kawaguchi 2016).

Compared to the artificial intelligence systems that see faeces in clouds, the "Internet of Shit" is a more atavistic version of the *crab in, crap out* principle described in the previous chapter (Steyerl in this volume), since it is only about the endless multiplication of dumb and wasteful electronic gadgets. But whether crapularity or singularity, the differentiation of systems into such subcategories as "internet," "artificial intelligence," "machine vision" and "pattern recognition," "Big Data," "smart cities," and "internet of things" will likely soon become a thing of the past. These systems are converging in the same way in which Hans Magnus Enzensberger, in 1970, predicted the convergence of communication media— "news satellites, color television, cable relay television, cassettes, videotape, videotape recorders, video-phones, stereophony, laser techniques, electrostatic reproduction processes, electronic high-speed printing, composing and learning machines, microfiches with electronic access, printing by radio, time-sharing computers, data banks"—into "a universal system" (Enzensberger 2003, 261). What sounded monumental then has now become banal, as could eventually be the case with the future convergence of analytics systems. Besides rendering obsolete such differentiations as those between Big Data, A.I., and smart cities, it is also likely to render obsolete the term "media" itself. The issue that information ceases to be a "difference which makes a difference" (Bateson 1972, 459) within technology is as old as McLuhan's definition of media as "extensions of man," (McLuhan 1964), which lacks any meaningful differentiation between "media" and other types of technology.

Fluxus showed, in 1962, how social network analytics and "social credit" can be computed using almost any technology, including the cheapest computational device of manual counting. In a 2004 interview with the curator Hans-Ulrich Obrist, Emmett Williams recalled how the artists disguised their control device as a friendly game. Counting audience members, Williams explains, meant that "you could touch them; you could have them write their names on the program, put a candy in everybody's mouth. This way you had contact with the audience and at the same time could work out exactly how many people were there and demand our fair share of the money" (Obrist, Arsène-Henry, and Shumon Basar 2010, n.p.). Contemporary design calls this "gamification," and it has become a widely practiced method for creating "soft" or "nudging" control measures in public and private spaces.[11]

A Fluxus score written a year before the first Fluxus festival, La Monte Young's *Compositions 1961* consisted only of the instruction to "Draw a straight line and follow it," (Young 1962) thus anticipating the singularity of a society whose architectures and processes have been streamlined and simplified, even "zombified," in order to be fully readable and serviceable by dumb bots. If machine-readability and human-readability, capture and analytics (as opposed to perception and interpretation), mark the difference between the "humanistic concept of knowledge" (Drucker 2011) and A.I., then this difference reveals a fundamental problem of A.I.: its very concept is, to use a term from speculative realist philosophy, *correlationist,* since the word *artificial* dialectically references *natural.* The quality standard for A.I., and the "singularity" as predicted by its advocates, is how convincingly it measures up against natural (i.e., human, partly also animal) intelligence.

Since there is no firm definition or universally agreed-upon scientific theory of "intelligence," one could just as well define intelligence as the capability to perform mathematical equations. Then, the singularity would already have been reached with pocket calculators, or even with some mechanical entrance-gate device that would had counted Fluxus festival visitors more efficiently than the *Counting Songs* did.[12] The Faroese musician and artist Goodiepal, who from 2004 to 2008 taught his students at the Danish Institute for Electroacoustic Music (DIEM) to compose music *for* alien and artificial intelligences,[13] therefore proposes to read A.I. not as an acronym for "artificial" but for "alternative intelligence." If machine intelligence is indeed a different form of intelligence, then it can be observed and judged on the basis of its own merits, as opposed to a messianic waiting for a moment where it might equal or eclipse (weakly defined) human intelligence. This would even render obsolete the question as to whether or not machines can think—which in itself willfully glosses over the corresponding opposite question, "Can humans think?" posed by the former Fluxus artist (and Emmett Williams collaborator) Tomas Schmit in the year 2000 (Schmit et al. 2007, 18–19).

The singularity is here, whether in counting songs, pocket calculators, or more sophisticated computational devices. But it is doomed to be a crapularity as these systems are increasingly layered on top of each other and kept running without maintenance, often even without anybody around who still knows how they work. This crappiness (which includes crappy Big Data "analytics") could be celebrated and enjoyed like other crappy culture, including television shows such as *NUMB3RS* and B movies such as *Space Truckers.* The problem, however, is that the crapularity is not a movie but has become daily life and that its worst jokes are actually deadly.

Negative Theologies of the Subject

While A.I. has become "alternative intelligence," the critical theory that Habermas defended against empirical positivism no longer seems to embody the human "alternative intelligence" that it was in the twentieth century. *Why,* Hito Steyerl asked the author of the present text, *can one analyze fascism all day long and no one cares?*[14] No one cares, it should be added, whether such analysis happens under Marxist or post-Marxist, feminist, postcolonial, poststructuralist, fundamental-ontological or object-oriented ontological, media-theoretical, speculative-realist, humanist or posthumanist denominations, since positivism boils all of these down to one undifferentiated "continental," "nonempirical" and "speculative" discourse.

In the crapularity, "subjectivity" gains a renewed significance as soon as this subjectivity is no longer an issue of metaphysical versus ontological thinking but more generally of criticism versus positivism. With her insistence on the "graphical expression of humanistic interpretation" as distinct from "the visual display of quantitative information as a close reading of a poem is from the chart of an eye tracker following movements across a printed page," Drucker (2011) shows how the word *humanistic* can be salvaged even for those kinds of cultural and media studies that have been thoroughly informed by poststructuralism and subsequent schools of antimetaphysical thinking.

Before the crapularity, any inclusion of "subjectivity" in "terms of media"—or more precisely, in information technology—seemed to be an oxymoron, since rejection (or at least criticism) of the humanist subject has been a common denominator of cybernetics, poststructuralism, and most schools of materialism and feminism (Braidotti 2013). The focus of media theory on technologies, rather than on their human creators, may in itself be seen as an antihumanist statement. Terry Eagleton's characterization of structuralism thus broadly applies to most media theory: it "is 'anti-humanist,' which means not that its devotees rob children of their sweets but that they reject the myth that meaning begins and ends in the individual's 'experience'" (Eagleton 1996, 98). This intellectual tradition began with Darwin's and Freud's shattering of the subject's autonomy and continued after the Second World War with cybernetics. In its close relatedness to psychological behaviorism, cybernetics understood human behavior as situated within control systems. In 1946, Heidegger—who was in the process of "turning"[15] his fundamental ontology into a philosophy of technology—stated that "every humanism remains metaphysical" and as such obstructs ontological inquiry, even of humanity itself.[16] What was primarily meant as clarification of Heidegger's philosophy in opposition to Sartre and his humanist misreading of Heidegger's existential philosophy[17] had a lasting impact on French poststructuralism and the media theory that subsequently borrowed from it.

When Michel Foucault declared the "death of man" in *Order of Things* (1966),[18] the death of God did not mean, as it did for humanism, his replacement by the human subject, but rather the death of the Christian god as well as of the humanist god-like subject. Kittler's lifelong "exorcism of humanism from the humanities," in which technology took the place of the historical subject, built upon Foucault while battling the remains of nineteenth-century idealism in continental European humanities (Kittler 1980). Antihumanism became posthumanism when poststructuralist dystopias turned into cyber-utopias. Donna Haraway's *Cyborg Manifesto* and N. Katherine Hayles's *How We Became Posthuman* examined A.I. and Silicon Valley culture from the angle of critical theory. Posthumanism turned what once had been negative theology into new utopias and new forms of gnosis.[19] Contemporary critiques of correlationism (Meillassoux 2009) and debates on the Anthropocene amount to a contemporary comeback of posthumanism, with a systems thinking that has shifted from 1990s cyber-utopias to twenty-first-century ecological dystopias (Braidotti 2013).

Did the antitheologies of "the subject" simply create new theologies of "the system"? The poststructuralist critique of subjectivity was more differentiated than it is often given credit for. In *What Is an Author?* Michel Foucault states that "suspicions arise concerning the absolute nature and creative role of the subject" while also insisting that "the subject should not be entirely abandoned. It should be reconsidered, not to restore the theme of an originating subject, but to seize its functions, its intervention in discourse, and its system of dependencies" (Foucault 2001, 1635). Subjectivity, in other words, is relative rather than absolute (as was previously the case in humanism and romanticism).[20]

The inscription of subjectivity into media—of perspective and pictures, whether or not machine vision is involved—needs no explanation when algorithmic processes produce racial, social, and other biases. Most engineers might consider these an optimization problem, an issue of the platonic ideal of singularity versus its crapularity in real life. Yet everyone who has ever coded a computer program, programmed a database, or marked up a document knows that this constantly involves subjective decisions:[21] for example, the criteria according to which input data is classified, sorted, and categorized, including the multiple-choice values for a person's gender in an address database, or the interpretation of italic type as either "emphasis" ("<em>") or "citation" ("<cite>") when transcribing text from print to HTML. No algorithmic analytics can sensibly accomplish the latter; it will only be able to compute and heuristically apply the statistical norm. "If you want a vision of the future, imagine the past (artificially) extended forever"—this line from the 1986 zine *SMILE* (which had the unusual characteristic that anyone could publish a zine under the name *SMILE*), written by the artist and later internet entrepreneur John Berndt under the multiple-use pseudonym Karen Eliot, is an precognitive summary of the crapularity and its analytics (Eliot 2010).

However, programmed systems also help to define more precisely what exactly differentiates "semantics" from "syntax" and interpretation from formal analysis. They thus bring to hermeneutics and structuralism, which only had vague definitions of these terms, an understanding of what these words really mean. Figures of speech, for example, can now be clearly understood as being subject to an interpretation that is difficult or impossible to formalize. Ambiguity and figurative speech mark the limits of what computer algorithms can analyze. Are Abwärts's "Computerstaat" lyrics an affirmative, oppositional, or cynical political statement? Even A.I. algorithms that determine the degree to which a statement is ironic based on semantic context would be thrown off track.[22]

Twentieth-century structuralists such as Roman Jakobson still thought of figures of speech as a formal aspect of language, since

they could be structurally described; a metaphor, for example,
could be understood as a linguistic operation based on the
principle of similarity (Jakobson 1956). Metaphor was classified as
"formal" because it could be made part of a systematics. Jakobson,
and later twentieth-century antihumanism, thus maintained
the romanticist notion of "subjectivity" as being antithetical to
systems, discourses, and apparatuses. In the crapularity, however,
subjectivity needs to be deromanticized. It can be simply defined
as the agency and decisions—in other words, politics—that make
up these systems, discourses, and apparatuses. To deny that these
politics exist would be an extremist, if not fascist, form of posthumanism advocating postpolitics and postdemocracy (Crouch 2004).

The Invisible Hand of Openness

If the Fluxus *Counting Songs* were performed by a machine, running
forever as an autonomous, unobserved process, this wouldn't take
away the human agency and politics that went into their design.
But their potential automation illustrates, perhaps counterintui-
tively, the degree to which they are an open process—or, to use
Umberto Eco's term, an "open work" characterized by an internal
"dialectics between work and openness" (Eco 1989, 104). For Eco,
this dialectic is one of the traditional material characteristics of
an artwork, which it still retains in order to remain dialectical, as
opposed to its modern-art processuality, for example in action
painting (102). In the case of the *Counting Songs,* this would be its
dialectics between (fixed) notation and (open) performance. Yet,
as previously discussed, the *closure* (in the sense of nonopenness)
of the *Counting Songs* lies in its implicit assumptions about the
situation—the kind of closure that would make a crapularity bot
stoically perform the *Counting Songs* in a heap of postnuclear
ruins, counting people while they are being shot dead by drones,
rendering the sum outdated even as it is being computed. Pattern
discrimination as it is applied in data and network analytics suffers
from this issue, since it boils down to applying predefined models
to an alleged mass—and mess—of contingent phenomena and

information, regardless of whether this information happens to be airport surveillance camera images, petabytes of intercepted emails, the sensor data of a "smart city," or the visitors of a Fluxus festival.

But whatever the type of analytics or interpretation involved, these necessarily rely on operation upon "the open," even if these "great outdoors"[23] are increasingly difficult to find (see Steyerl in this volume); and regardless of the fact that the analytics in question are limited to seeing only what the search and correlation methods will tell them to see—not to mention the risk of a crapularity bot data-mining minefields even as they are blowing up. "Openness" is where analytics and hermeneutics meet: "open data," the sibling of Big Data, and "open work" both imply an antischolastics of rejecting precategorized and prehierarchized knowledge. When hermeneutics was still a theological discipline, its mere existence implied that the meaning of the scripture (whether Torah, Bible, or Qur'an) was not literal and fixed, as the orthodoxies and fundamentalisms of the monotheistic religions hold, but rather subject to interpretation and, over the course of time, reinterpretation. This process not only secularized scripture but also hermeneutics itself so that, by the nineteenth century, it had mutated into literary criticism (Schleiermacher 1998).

In the 1960s and 1970s, Eco was not the only literary theoretician to modernize hermeneutics and literary criticism, and to make "openness" (in the sense of open work as well as open interpretation) the key factor in this modernization. Roland Barthes advocated the "networks" and "galaxy of signifiers" in the "indeterminable" codes of the "writerly" text (Barthes 1974, 5), while Wolfgang Iser and Hans-Robert Jauss (building on previous work by Roman Ingarden) proposed a reader-response hermeneutics that focused on the gaps that artworks leave for their readers' imagination (Iser 1978). While these theories only addressed the aesthetics—perception—rather than the media technology of text, they were nevertheless misread as technology blueprints in the hypertext literature criticism that to some extent preceded, and further accompanied the emergence of the World Wide Web in the early 1990s.[24] Around the same time, activism to make and keep the internet an "open" medium began in grassroots initiatives such as the Electronic Frontier Foundation. By the late 1990s and early 2000s, the concept of openness was extended to software (open source) and other media (open content), as well as academic publishing (open access) and data (open data).

From Eco's *Open Work* in 1962 to the *Open Government Data* definition in 2007 (Fretwell 2014), "open" thus always meant "good" or at least "more interesting." Openness provides more value for interpretation, whether for literary philologists or real-estate app developers using open government data to assess the potential market value of a neighborhood. For philologists as well as app developers, interpretative value translates into economic value as it helps keep them in business. (In this light, claims of the imminent "end of work" seem exaggerated.[25]) Both "open work" hermeneutics and open data analytics presuppose a culture and society that enables them while preventing closure (nonopenness) through orthodoxy. They are thus close cousins to Popper's general concept of the "open society" (Popper 1945). Projected from science onto politics, Popper's principle of falsification turns this open society into a market of competing ideas that are given the opportunity to prove each other wrong. On a dystopian level, this also creates a business model for the age of crapularity. Since falsification never ends (as opposed to Hegel's and Marx's historical dialectics), it amounts to an infinite license for the crapularity to carry on with crap analytics, crap results, and crappy technology, keeping culture and society in a state of permanent system updates, error messages, and software-dependency hells where doors stop working because their remote control apps are no longer being maintained and where two bugs are fixed by introducing ten new ones.[26]

Popper's open society, however, is not radically open since it still differentiates between itself and "its enemies": fascism, soviet communism, and their alleged precursors in political-philosophical utopias. If "open societies" need enemies in order to be defined, it is not surprising that nowadays these enemies include the *extraterritorial enclaves and duty-free gated communities, para-statelets and anti-"terrorist" operation zones, offshore entities and corporate proxy concessions* described in the previous chapter (Steyerl in this volume).

The "open society" is, in other words, only open to the degree to which its fundamental system is not challenged. Openness thus only exists on the object level of what is being observed, not on the metalevel of the observation where the organizing principle, "open society," remains as fixed as the scores of "open works" such as the *Counting Songs.* Whenever "open" is used as a term to describe media—such as in open standards, open networks, open source, open access, open data—then the same logic of immutability remains at work. Openness is standardized in policy documents (such as the *Open Source Definition* [Open Source Initiative 1998], the eight criteria of Open Government Data [OpenGovData.org 2007], the *Open Content Definition* [Wiley 1998], "gold" and "green" open access and the comprehensive *Open Definition* [Open Definition 2015]) making all these "terms of media" compliant to, and cybernetic heirs of, the Popperian liberal politics equation of open science, open markets, and open society.

The myth underlying both these politics and the overall concept of open systems is their inherent self-regulation toward "thermodynamic equilibrium" and "equifinality" toward a "steady state" of a system, to quote Popper's correspondent, the biologist and founder of General Systems Theory Ludwig von Bertalanffy (Bertalanffy 1969). For Popper and Bertalanffy, these principles amounted to a general model of science, nature, and politics in the Cold War period. Ultimately, they are riffs on Adam Smith's "invisible hand." In a founding manifesto for the open source movement, the software developer Eric S. Raymond summed up this ideology as follows: "The Linux world behaves in many respects like a free market or an ecology, a collection of selfish agents attempting to maximize utility which in the process produces a self-correcting spontaneous order more elaborate and efficient than any amount of central planning could have achieved" (Raymond 1998). Tuned for equilibrium and self-regulation, the system is thus not open in the sense of being contingent or indeterministic; instead, it is meant to produce a desired outcome, with what one could call "liberal" variations. The same logic applies to "open work," including aleatory musical composition, action painting, participatory art such as the *Counting Songs* (with their desired outcome of knowing the number of paying visitors), and contemporary community art and social design.

The People against Posthumanism

For Popper's open society and for open source software, the desired outcomes were a better society and better software, respectively, through systemic processes that are by design self-organizing and self-optimizing.[27] But just as the *Counting Songs* cease to produce sensible outcomes in a postapocalyptic world and end up as no more than a formula running amok, open source software ended up as the technological back end of the crapularity, with Linux, Apache, MySQL, and PHP driving the commercial web and mobile devices (including, to name just a few examples, Google's search engine, Gmail, YouTube, Facebook's social networking platforms, Amazon's online retail store, Android smartphones and tablets, Google's Chromebooks, the Kindle e-reader, and Tesla's autopilot). The "open society" is now better known under the name coined by Popper's Mont Pelerin Society collaborator Alexander Rüstow, "neoliberalism,"[28] which has historically proven to be able to falsify anything but itself.

This explains the resurgence of fascism and other forms of populism in the context of the crapularity. On the basis of Carl Schmitt's political theology, populism offers a more honest alternative to the existing regime: against equilibrium promises and crapular reality, the proposed antidote is the state of exception; against invisible hands, the remedy is decision making as a virtue in itself, what Schmitt referred to as "decisionism."[29] In other words, the states of exception and decisionism that various "systems" (from international political treaties to Big Data analytics) and postdemocratic powers currently conceal seem to become tangible and accountable again through populist reembodiment. "Populism" could be literally read as the will to power against "the system," not only a specific system but the concept of system as such (including the way in which Popper's "open society" positions itself). Contemporary populism is an attempt to regain agency of people against posthuman ecologies, to literally put up the *demos,* the body of the people, against crapularities—whether on occupied squares or at fascist campaign rallies.

The tragedy, or farce, of this confrontation is how it often ends up as one form of fascism against another: populist fascism against Big Data fascism. The algorithm that stigmatizes people of color with a higher crime risk and a lower credit score differs from a white supremacist—or in continental Europe, "identitarian"—street rally only in its symbolic form, not in its semantics and pragmatics. Both can be based on the same crapularity analytics, since today's populist street rallies are often the outcome of algorithms that bring like-minded people together in online social media echo chambers. Either way, subjectivity is destined to remain hard-coded into this analytics, even after humanity is literally (and not just figuratively) dead and gone.

Notes

For Rasheedah, Camae, and Ras

1   And also turned certain analysts into another kind of analyst: some languages, including German, now differentiate between "Analytiker," a psychotherapeutic, philosophical, or mathematical analyst, and "Analyst," a stock market, business, or data analyst.

2   I am reusing a term coined by Linda Hilfling Ritasdatter for the accompanying symposium to her exhibition *Bugs in the War Room* at Overgarden, Copenhagen, Denmark, May 2016, and for her ongoing PhD research on the 2K bug and the legacy programming language Algol.

3   "Deutschland Katastrophenstaat / Wir leben im Computerstaat / Wir leben im Computerstaat / Wir leben im Computerstaat" (Abwärts 1980).

4   It would be worthwhile to research possible correlations between the surge in police shootings of black people since 2014 and the introduction of predictive

policing programs in the United States (on the other hand, the availability of inexpensive media technology has surely increased the coverage of previously unreported incidents, so that correlations are difficult to draw). In their 2016 paper "Police Killings of Unarmed Black People: Centering Race and Racism in Human Behavior and the Social Environment Content," the social work researchers Willie F. Tolliver, Bernadette R. Hadden, Fabienne Snowden, and Robyn Brown-Manning argue that "the passage of laws like 'stand your ground' joined with policing strategies such as 'broken windows,' 'stop and frisk,' and 'predictive policing' (Eligon and Williams 2015) results in Black and Brown people being exposed to surveillance by police, vigilantes, and the general public."

5   Autobiographical note: the German edition of this book, published in 1984, introduced the author of the present text to network computing and its criticism.

6   A similar dispute existed in 1950s American political science over the school of behavioralism (not to be confused with behaviorism) whose advocacy for an empirical approach of "verification," "quantification," and "pure science" was critiqued and rejected by Bernard Crick (1959), among others.

7   "Die Erkenntnis beginnt nicht mit Wahrnehmungen oder Beobachtungen oder der Sammlung von Daten oder von Tatsachen, sondern sie beginnt mit *Problemen.*"

8   Today's optical sensor technology cannot capture the full range of color information present, for example, in Kodachrome slides and film negatives; therefore digitization requires a decision regarding the color gamut to be captured. After scanning, the captured color range needs to be additionally, and quite heavily, compressed in order to fit the even more limited color space and dynamic range of computer displays.

9   "Film emulsions could have been designed initially with more sensitivity to the continuum of yellow, brown, and reddish skin tones, but the design process would have had to be motivated by a recognition of the need for an extended dynamic range. At the time film emulsions were developing, the target consumer market would have been 'Caucasians' in a segregated political scene" (Roth 2009, 118).

10 A less rigorous version of this program was carried out in the redesign of Western cities to make them car friendly after the Second World War.

11 A good example are the welcome gifts handed out by public service workers to newborn children in some European countries; this also serves as a measure of identity control.

12 See Bruno Latour's related discussion of the doorstop as a nonhuman actor performing a previously human task, in Latour 2005, 14–41.

13 "I wanted to teach my students how to make music for an artificial intelligence in the future, but I was told I was not allowed to do that. I said if I cannot do that I will leave. And I will not leave silently. This is academic war!" Goodiepal in an interview by Aram Yardumian (2012).

14 Hito Steyerl's comment to the first draft of this paper.

15 German: "Kehre"

16 "In defining the humanity of the human being, humanism not only does not ask

about the relation of being to the essence of the human being; because of its metaphysical origin humanism even impedes the question by neither recognizing nor understanding it" (Heidegger 1998, 245).

17 German: "Existenzphilosophie"

18 "It is no longer possible to think in our day other than in the void left by man's disappearance. For this void does not create a deficiency; it does not constitute a lacuna that must be filled. It is nothing more, and nothing less, than the unfolding of a space in which it is once more possible to think" (Foucault 2002, 373).

19 Haraway (2003, 192) writes that there is a "utopian tradition of imagining a world without gender"; while Hayles argues that "cybernetics . . . should be called a 'Manichean science'" (Hayles 1999, 106).

20 In Speculative Realism, objects conversely become independent from the human perspective, they are no longer "correlationist." Slavoj Žižek criticizes this position to the extent that "the true problem is not to think pre-subjective reality, but to think how something like a subject could have emerged within it; without this (properly Hegelian) gesture, any objectivism will remain correlationist in a hidden way—its image of 'reality in itself' remains correlated (even if in a negative way) with subjectivity". Like Drucker, Žižek insists on the human perspective when he states (referring to Lacan and Hegel) that "their problem is not 'how to reach objective reality which is independent of (its correlation to) subjectivity,' but how subjectivity is already inscribed into reality—to quote Lacan again, not only is the picture in my eye, but I am also in the picture" (Žižek 2012, 643).

21 In 2001, the artist and computer programmer Adrian Ward summed up this issue as follows: "we should be thinking about embedding our own creative subjectivity into automated systems, rather than naively trying to get a robot to have its 'own' creative agenda. A lot of us do this day in, day out. We call it programming" (Ward 2001).

22. The algorithm proposed by Amir et al. (2016) depends on strong contextual cues from unambiguous (social media) messages.

23 "le grand dehors" (Meillassoux 2009).

24 Most prominently in Landow 1992.

25 As opposed to Black 1986 and Srnicek and Williams 2015.

26 Philip K. Dick anticipated this type of crapularity in his 1969 novel *Ubik,* in which a character struggles with a door in his apartment that refuses to open unless it is paid with coins and ultimately threatens to sue him because he tries to unscrew its lock (Dick 1991, 24).

27 According to the Open Source Initiative (2016), "the promise of open source [is]: higher quality, greater reliability, more flexibility, lower cost, and an end to predatory vendor lock-in." In the past, the organization's rhetoric showed an even more optimistic attitude, praising, in 2006 and on the same web page, open source for software development "at a speed that, if one is used to the slow pace of conventional software development, seems astonishing," with a "rapid evolutionary process" that "produces better software than the traditional closed model. . . . Open source software is an idea whose time has finally

come. . . . Now it's breaking out into the commercial world, and that's changing all the rules" (Open Source Initiative 2006).

28 Rüstow understood "neoliberalism" as a synonym of "ordoliberalism," the German (and Northern European) concept of a market liberalism tempered by a strong system of checks and balances enforced by the state, including provisions for public welfare. He eventually left the Mont Pelerin Society in disagreement with proponents of radical free market liberalism (Prollius 2007).

29 Schmitt 1985. See also Mouffe 1999.

References

Abwärts. 1980. *Abwärts—Computerstaat*. Vinyl 7". Hamburg: ZickZack. Audio recording.

Amir, Silvio, Byron C. Wallace, Hao Lyu, and Paula Carvalho Mário J. Silva. 2016. "Modelling Context with User Embeddings for Sarcasm Detection in Social Media." *arXiv:1607.00976 [Cs]*, July 4. Accessed January 19, 2017. http://arxiv.org/abs/1607.00976.

Angwin, Julia. 2016. "Make Algorithms Accountable." *The New York Times*, August 1. Accessed January 19, 2017. http://www.nytimes.com/2016/08/01/opinion/make-algorithms-accountable.html.

Angwin, Julia, Jeff Larson, Surya Mattu, and Lauren Kirchner. 2016. "Machine Bias: There's Software Used Across the Country to Predict Future Criminals. And It's Biased against Blacks." *ProPublica*, May 23. Accessed January 19, 2017. https://www.propublica.org/article/machine-bias-risk-assessments-in-criminal-sentencing.

arXiv, Emerging Technology from the. 2016. "Neural Networks Are Inadvertently Learning Our Language's Hidden Gender Biases." *MIT Technology Review*, July 27. Accessed July 30, 2016. https://www.technologyreview.com/s/602025/how-vector-space-mathematics-reveals-the-hidden-sexism-in-language/.

Barthes, Roland. 1974. *S/Z*. New York: Hill and Wang.

Bateson, Gregory. 1972. *Steps to an Ecology of Mind*. Chicago: University of Chicago Press.

Bertalanffy, Ludwig von. 1969. *General System Theory: Foundations, Development, Applications*. New York: George Braziller.

Black, Bob. 1986. *The Abolition of Work and Other Essays*. Port Townsend, Wash.: Loompanics Unlimited.

Braidotti, Rosi. 2013. *The Posthuman*. Cambridge: Polity Press.

Cayley, John. 2012. "Terms of Reference and Vectoralist Transgressions: Situating Certain Literary Transactions over Networked Services." *Amodern 2: Network Archaeology*. Accessed July 27, 2016. http://amodern.net/article/terms-of-reference-vectoralist-transgressions/#rf21-2020.

Chun, Wendy Hui Kyong. 2016. *Updating to Remain the Same: Habitual New Media*. Cambridge, Mass.: The MIT Press.

Crawford, Kate. 2016. "A.I.'s White Guy Problem." *The New York Times*, June 25. Accessed July 30, 2016. https://www.nytimes.com/2016/06/26/opinion/sunday/artificial-intelligences-white-guy-problem.html.

56   Crick, Bernard. 1959. *The American Science of Politics: Its Origins and Conditions*. Berkeley: University of California Press.

Crouch, Colin. 2004. *Post-Democracy*. Malden, Mass.: Polity.

Dick, Philip K. 1991. *Ubik*. New York: Vintage Books.

Drucker, Johanna. 2011. "Humanities Approaches to Graphical Display." *digital humanities quarterly* 5, no. 1. Accessed July 30, 2016. http://www.digitalhumanities .org/dhq/vol/5/1/000091/000091.html.

Eagleton, Terry. 1996. *Literary Theory: An Introduction*. Minneapolis: University of Minnesota Press.

Eco, Umberto. 1989. *The Open Work*. Cambridge, Mass.: Harvard University Press.

Eligon, John, and Timothy Williams. 2015. "Police Program Aims to Pinpoint Those Most Likely to Commit Crimes." *The New York Times,* September 24. Accessed July 30, 2016. http://www.nytimes.com/2015/09/25/us/police-program-aims-to-pin point-those-most-likely-to-commit-crimes.html.

Eliot, Karen. 2010. "ANTI-POST-ACTUALISM++++++." *A Neoist Research Project,* ed. N. O. Cantsin. London: OpenMute.

Enzensberger, Hans Magnus. 2003. "Constituents of a Theory of the Media." In *The New Media Reader,* ed. Noah Wardrip-Fruin and Nick Montfort, 261–75. Cambridge, Mass.: MIT Press.

Foucault, Michel. 2001. "What Is an Author?" In *The Norton Anthology of Theory and Criticism,* ed. Vincent B. Leitch, 1622–36. New York: Norton.

Foucault, Michel. 2002. *The Order of Things: An Archaeology of the Human Sciences.* Oxford: Psychology Press.

Fretwell, Luke. 2014. "A Brief History of Open Data." *FCW: The Business of Federal Technology,* June 9. Accessed January 19, 2017. https://fcw.com/articles/2014/06/09/ exec-tech-brief-history-of-open-data.aspx.

Gordon, Stuart. 1997. *Space Truckers*. Film.

Groys, Boris. 2016. *In the Flow*. London: Verso.

Habermas, Jürgen. 1976. "The Analytical Theory of Science and Dialectics: A Postscript to the Controversy between Popper and Adorno." In *The Positivist Dispute in German Sociology,* ed. Theodor W. Adorno, Hans Albert, Ralf Dahrendorf, Jürgen Habermas, Harald Pilot, and Karl R. Popper and trans Glyn Adey and David Frisby, 131–62. London: Heinemann.

Haraway, Donna. 2003. "The Cyborg Manifesto." In *The New Media Reader,* ed. Noah Wardrip-Fruin and Nick Montfort, 515–42. Cambridge, Mass.: MIT Press.

Hatton, Celia. 2015. "China 'Social Credit': Beijing Sets up Huge System." *BBC News,* October 26. Accessed July 30, 2016. http://www.bbc.com/news/world-asia-china -34592186.

Hayles, N. Katherine. 1999. *How We Became Posthuman: Virtual Bodies in Cybernetics, Literature, and Informatics.* Chicago: University of Chicago Press.

Heidegger, Martin. 1998. *Pathmarks,* ed. William McNeill. Cambridge: Cambridge University Press.

Internet of Shit. 2015. "Internet of Shit (@internetofshit)." *Twitter*. Accessed January 19, 2017. https://twitter.com/internetofshit.

Iser, Wolfgang. 1978. *The Act of Reading: A Theory of Aesthetic Response.* Baltimore: The Johns Hopkins University Press.

Jakobson, Roman. 1956. "Two Aspects of Language and Two Types of Aphasic Disturbances." In *Fundamentals of Language,* ed. Roman Jakobson and Morris Halle, 115–33. The Hague and Paris: Mouton.

Kawaguchi, Kohsuke. 2016. "Over the Air Update of a Toyota Car in Progress While the Car Is Driving. Wow!" *Microblog @kohsukekawa, Twitter,* July 8. Accessed July 9, 2016. pic.twitter.com/54hMOr27Bj.

Kittler, Friedrich, ed. 1980. *Austreibung des Geistes aus den Geisteswissenschaften: Programme des Poststrukturalismus.* Paderborn/Munich/Vienna/Zurich: Schöningh.

Kurzweil, Ray. 2005. *The Singularity Is Near: When Humans Transcend Biology.* New York: Viking.

Landow, George P. 1992. *Hypertext: The Convergence of Contemporary Critical Theory and Technology.* Baltimore: The Johns Hopkins University Press.

Latour, Bruno. 2005. "From Realpolitik to Dingpolitik or How to Make Things Public." In *Making Things Public: Atmospheres of Democracy,* 14–41. Cambridge, Mass.: MIT Press.

Levin, Sam, and Nicky Woolf. 2016. "Tesla Driver Killed While Using Autopilot Was Watching Harry Potter, Witness Says." *The Guardian,* July 1. Accessed July 1, 2016. https://www.theguardian.com/technology/2016/jul/01/tesla-driver-killed-autopilot -self-driving-car-harry-potter.

McLuhan, Marshall. 1964. *Understanding Media: The Extensions of Man.* New York: McGraw-Hill.

Meillassoux, Quentin. 2009. *After Finitude: An Essay on the Necessity of Contingency.* London: Continuum.

Mouffe, Chantal. 1999. *The Challenge of Carl Schmitt.* London: Verso.

Northpointe. 2016. "Northpointe—About Us." Official website. Accessed January 19, 2017. http://www.northpointeinc.com/about-us.

Obrist, Hans-Ulrich, Charles Arsène-Henry, and Shumon Basar, eds. 2010. *Hans Ulrich Obrist: Interviews, Volume 2.* Milan: Charta Art.

Open Definition. 2015. "Open Definition 2.1." *Open Definition.* Accessed August 1, 2016. http://opendefinition.org/od/2.1/en/.

OpenGovData.org. 2007. "The 8 Principles of Open Government Data." *OpenGovData. org.* Accessed August 1, 2016. https://opengovdata.org.

Open Source Initiative. 1998. "The Open Source Definition (Annotated)." *Open Source Initiative.* Accessed January 19, 2017. https://opensource.org/osd-annotated.

Open Source Initiative. 2006. Official website. Accessed through the Internet Archive Wayback Machine, August 1, 2016. https://web.archive.org/web/20060207222246/ http://www.opensource.org/.

Open Source Initiative. 2016. Official website. Accessed January 19, 2017. https:// opensource.org/.

Popper, Karl R. 1945. *The Open Society and Its Enemies.* London: G. Routledge & Sons, Ltd.

Popper, Karl R. 1962. "Die Logik Der Sozialwissenschaften." *Kölner Zeitschrift Für Soziologie und Sozialpsychologie* 14, no. 2: 233–48.

Prollius, Michael von. 2007. *Herrschaft oder Freiheit: Ein Alexander-Rüstow-Brevier.* Bern: Hep Ott.

Raford, Noah, John A. Sweeney, Justin Pickard, et al. *Alternatives to the Singularity* [collaborative manuscript], 2011. http://www.scribd.com/doc/62056338/Alterna tives-to-the-Singularity. Accessed through the Internet Wayback Machine, June 17, 2017. https://web.archive.org/web/20120916123714/http://www.scribd.com/ doc/62056338/Alternatives-to-the-Singularity.

Raymond, Eric S. 1998. "The Cathedral and the Bazaar." *Catb.org*. Accessed January 19, 2017. http://www.catb.org/esr/writings/cathedral-bazaar/cathedral-bazaar/ ar01s11.html.

Roth, Lorna. 2009. "Looking at Shirley, the Ultimate Norm: Colour Balance, Image Technologies, and Cognitive Equity." *Canadian Journal of Communication* 34, no. 1: 111–36.

Schleiermacher, Friedrich. 1998. *Hermeneutics and Criticism and Other Writings,* ed. Andrew Bowie. Cambridge: Cambridge University Press.

Scott, Ridley. 2002. *Black Hawk Down.* Film.

Scott, Tony. 1986. *Top Gun.* Film.

Scott, Tony. 1998. *Enemy of the State.* Film.

Scott, Ridley, and Tony Scott. 2005–2010. "NUMB3RS." *TV Series.* Los Angeles: CBS.

Schmit, Tomas, Julia Friedrich, Museum Ludwig, and Sammlung Falckenberg. 2007. *Tomas Schmit: Können Menschen Denken? = Are Humans Capable of Thought?* Cologne: Museum Ludwig/Verlag der Buchhandlung Walther König.

Schmitt, Carl. 1985. *Political Theology: Four Chapters on the Concept of Sovereignty.* Chicago: University of Chicago Press.

Sohm, Hanns, Harald Szeemann, and Kölnischer Kunstverein. 1970. *Happening & Fluxus: Materialien.* Cologne: Kölnischer Kunstverein.

Srnicek, Nick, and Alex Williams. 2015. *Inventing the Future: Postcapitalism and a World without Work.* London: Verso.

Tolliver, Willie F., Bernadette R. Hadden, Fabienne Snowden, and Robyn Brown-Manning. 2016. "Police Killings of Unarmed Black People: Centering Race and Racism in Human Behavior and the Social Environment Content." *Journal of Human Behavior in the Social Environment* 26, no. 3–4 (2016): 279–86. Taylor and Francis+NEJM.

Vallee, Jacques. 1982. *The Network Revolution: Confessions of a Computer Scientist.* Berkeley: And/Or Press.

Verhoeven, Paul. 1987. *RoboCop.* Film.

Ward, Adrian, 2001. Posting to Rhizome mailing list. May 7.

Wiley, David. 1998. "Defining the 'Open' in Open Content and Open Educational Resources." *Opencontent.org*. Accessed January 19, 2017. http://www.opencontent .org/definition/.

Williams, Emmett. 1991. *My Life in Flux and Vice Versa.* Stuttgart/London/Reykjavik: Edition Hansjörg Mayer.

Yardumian, Aram. 2012. "A Gentleman's War." *Times Quotidian,* March 22. Accessed July 31, 2016. http://www.timesquotidian.com/2012/03/22/a-gentlemans-war/.

Young, La Monte. 1962. "Compositions 1961." *Fluxus* 1. New York: Fluxus Editions.

Žižek, Slavoj. 2012. *Less than Nothing: Hegel and the Shadow of Dialectical Materialism.* London: Verso, 2012.

3

Queerying Homophily

Wendy Hui Kyong Chun

To recap, in *Pattern Discrimination*:

1. YOU is always singular plural:
    - Recognition is never at the level of the individual
    - You = YOUS value

2. Machines engage in deep dreaming, creating patterns from noise.
    - Crab in = crap out
    - As with the gibbering muses, interpretation and hermeneutics enter through pattern discrimination, but now through the "back door"
    - We live in mythic times, but without knowing we do

3. The singularity of the market = the crapularity of the world:
    - the dumbing down of humans
    - the integration of subjectivity into information technologies
    - the reality of paranoia

4. To come out, we have to come in:
- we are inside when we think we are outside.
- Open societies need enemies to be "open"

This chapter continues these points by examining homophily—the axiom that similarity breeds connection—which grounds contemporary network science. If we are inside-out, it is because homophily, love as love of the same, closes the world it pretends to open; it makes cyberspace a series of echo chambers. This transformation ironically fulfills its purpose as a portal: a portal is an elaborate façade that frames the entrance to an enclosed space. Cyberspace was always a horizon trapped within in U.S. military-academic networks. Thus, to start with a more contemporary myth:

> *Once upon a time, a U.S. commerce-free, military, and academic inter-networking protocol, Transmission Control Protocol/Internet Protocol, became reborn as cyberspace. A consensual hallucination, it transformed TCP/IP into its opposite: a global, government-free, and anonymous space that was fundamentally discrimination-free (because if you can't see it, how can you hate it?). A decentralized network allegedly designed to survive a massive, catastrophic flattening (i.e., nuclear war), it would flatten all hierarchies through its boundless expansion. Unfortunately, things did not quite turn out as planned. Rather than an endless difference-free utopia, the internet became a series of poorly gated communities that spawned towering, hate- and terror-filled, racist— or to some even worse, banal, star-obsessed, cat-infested— echo chambers. This Internet made cyberpunk dystopian futures look banal in comparison. Rather than state-free, it became a breeding ground for state surveillance, in which governments spied on citizens, on foreign nationals, and on each other, and in which corporations perfected global tracking techniques. The future it augured looked even darker: the dusk of human spontaneity via the dawn of Big Data. Soon all human actions would be captured, calibrated, predicted,*

and preempted. Networks, it would seem, were born free and yet everywhere were enchained.

People bemoaned, accepted, or embraced this situation and offered various explanations for it. They revealed that the initial dreams of cyberspace were delusional (as if this was profound: the term "cyberspace," after all, came from science fiction; William Gibson in Neuromancer *described it as a "consensual hallucination"); they argued that the internet had to be purged of the anonymity (it never really had) because anonymity was the root of all evil (as if people were only obnoxious or nasty under cover); they pointed out that echo chambers were produced by "personalization": corporate attempts to target individual consumers. What we were experiencing: the nightmare of buying "happily ever after."*

This tale is both right and wrong. Yes, the internet changed dramatically after its opening/commercialization, but personalization alone is not the culprit—and purging the internet of anonymity will not make networks any less nasty. "Real Names" or unique identifiers lie at heart of Big Data analytics, for they are crucial to synching disparate databases and calibrating recycled data. Further, if Big Data predictive analytics work, it is not because everyone is treated like a special snowflake but because network analyses segregate users into "neighborhoods" based on their intense likes and dislikes. Further, it "trains" individuals to expect and recognize this segregation. Instead of ushering in a postracial, postidentitarian era, networks perpetuate identity via "default" variables and axioms. In network science, differences and similarities—differences as a way to shape similarities—are actively sought, shaped, and instrumentalized in order to apprehend network structures. Networks are neither unstructured masses nor endless rhizomes that cannot be cut or traced. Networks, because of their complexities, noisiness, and persistent inequalities, foster techniques to manage, prune, and predict. This new method—this pattern discrimination—makes older, deterministic, or classically analytic methods of control seem innocuous.

Homophily (love as love of the same) fuels pattern discrimination. The fact that networks perpetuate segregation should surprise no one because, again, segregation in the form of homophily lies at their conceptual core. Homophily launders hate into collective love, a transformation that, as Sara Ahmed has shown, grounds modern white supremacism (2004, 123). Homophily reveals and creates boundaries within theoretically flat and diffuse networks; it distinguishes and discriminates between allegedly equal nodes: it is a tool for discovering bias and inequality and for perpetuating it in the name of "comfort," predictability, and common sense. Network and data analyses compound and reflect discrimination embedded within society. Like the trolls Whitney Phillips has diagnosed as the "grimacing poster children for the socially networked world," they engage in "a grotesque pantomime of dominant cultural tropes" (2015, 8). Most broadly, this pattern discrimination is linked to a larger subsumption of democratic politics to neoliberal market economics, with its naïve overvaluing of openness (as discussed by Cramer in the preceding chapter) and authenticity (diagnosed brilliantly by Elizabeth Bernstein [2007]).

To intervene, we need to realize that this pantomime is not simply dramatic, it is also performative—it puts in place the world it discovers. It also depends on constantly repeated actions to create and sustain nodes and connections. We must thus embrace network analyses and work with network scientists to create new algorithms, new hypotheses, new grounding axioms. We also need to reembrace critical theory: feminism, ethnic studies, deconstruction, and yes, even psychoanalysis, data analytics' repressed parent. Most crucially, what everyone needs now: training in critical ethnic studies.

Machine Learning: Money Laundering for Bias?

On June 19, 2016, Pinboard—an account linked to a site advertised as "Social Bookmarking for Introverts"—posted the following comment to *Twitter*: "Machine learning is like money laundering for bias" (Pinboard 2016). This post, which was retweeted over a thousand times by the end of that summer, encapsulated growing suspicions about the objectivity of artificial intelligence and data-driven algorithms, suspicions confirmed by Cathy O'Neil in her remarkable *Weapons of Math Destruction: How Big Data Increases Inequality and Threatens Democracy* (2016). During this time period, news reports about biases embedded in machine learning abound-ed. Just two of the stories reported in the mainstream media the week of August 28, 2016, include news that:

- *Facebook* unexpectedly fired its news curators, in a de-layed response to allegations that its editors deliberately suppressed conservative news, charges it had previously denied (Thielman 2016). This resulted, as *the Guardian* reported, in the algorithms going "crazy." Among the top stories: a fraudulent one that then Fox News moderator Megyn Kelly was fired after she revealed that she was backing Hillary Clinton and a real video of a man mastur-bating with a McDonald's sandwich. According to some, this was because Facebook had not addressed the human problem embedded in machine algorithms: *Fortune* con-tended that "getting rid of human editors won't solve *Face-book*'s bias problem" because, in the end, the algorithms are written by human programmers (Ingram 2016).
- A coalition of civil liberties and civil rights organizations issued a statement against predictive policing technolo-gies. According to this group, the crime data embedded in these programs poisoned the results. This data is "notoriously suspect, incomplete, easily manipulated, and plagued by racial bias" (Lartey 2016). These allegations fol-lowed a report by *Upturn* that revealed that these systems are not only overhyped, they also "reinforce dispropor-tionate and discriminatory policing practices" (Robinson and Koepke 2016).

These are two of many. There are, as my coauthors have pointed out, many more instances of discriminatory algorithms. Other stories that broke in 2015–16 include news that:

- Google's photo app tagged two black people as "gorillas." Vivienne Ming, an artificial intelligence expert argued, "some systems struggle to recognize non-white people because they were trained on Internet images which are overwhelmingly white . . . the bias of the Internet reflects the bias of society." (Revealingly, Babak Hodjat, chief scientist at Sentinet Technologies, hypothesized that this error might have stemmed from the fact that the algorithm had not seen enough pictures of gorillas; Blarr 2015). This misrecognition of nonwhite people by cameras was hardly new: as Cramer also notes in his chapter in this volume, in 2009 it was revealed that HP Face-Tracking Webcams could not recognize black people, and the Nikon S360 asked its users if smiling Asians were "blinking" (see Frucci 2015; Lee 2009).
- The COMPAS software used by several U.S. courts to predict recidivism—and thus by some to determine sentencing and parole—was biased against racial minorities (Angwin et al. 2016).

These cases "revealed" well-documented biases that should not have been news. Historically, standard film stock was optimized for white skin; for the longest time, interracial filming was difficult not only for social reasons but also for technological ones (see Dyer 1997). As well, racial bias in sentencing within the United States has been debated and analyzed for years.[1] Further, racism within machine learning algorithms had been highlighted and predicted by numerous scholars: from Dr. Latanya Sweeney's revelation that "a black-identifying name was 25% more likely to get an ad suggestive of an arrest record" to predictions of price discrimination based on "social sorting"; from "inadvertent" and illegal discriminatory choices embedded in hiring software to biased risk profiles within terrorism-deterrence systems. These all highlighted the racism latent within seemingly objective systems, which, like money laundering, cleaned "crooked" data. To many, the solution was thus better, cleaner data: crime data, scrubbed free of police bias; more images of black folks in libraries; more diversity within the tech industry, so technologies not tested on minorities would not reach the consumer market (Harris 2016). The problem, in other words, was the still-lingering digital divide.

Other analysts, however, pointed out that it is not simply a question of inclusion or exclusion but also of how differences are "latently" encoded. For example, Chicago police did not use overtly racial categories in their predictive policing algorithm to generate a "heat list" of those most likely to murder or be murdered, because they did not need to: their "neighborhood"-based system effectively discriminated on the basis of race (Saunders, Hunt, and Hollywood 2016). This system created "persons of interest" based on social ties (as well as personal history). As Kate Crawford and Jason Schultz have argued, Big Data compromises privacy protections afforded by the U.S. legal system by making personally identifiable information about "protected categories" legible (Crawford and Schultz 2014). As Faiyaz Al Zamal et al. (2012) have shown in their analysis of Twitter, latent attributes such as age and political affiliation are easily inferred via a user's "neighbors." These algorithms, in other words, do not need to track racial and other differences, because these factors are already embedded in "less crude" categories designed to predict industriousness, reliability, homicidal tendencies, et cetera. These algorithms can more precisely target key intersectional identities. Tellingly, Christopher Wylie—the Cambridge Analytica whistle-blower—told the *Guardian*'s Carole Cadwalladr that Steven Bannon was the only straight man Wylie's ever talked to about feminist intersectional theory. Feminist intersectional theory was first developed by Kimberlé Crenshaw (Crenshaw 1991) to explain the violence against women of color—through Cambridge Analytica, it became a measure to understand "the oppressions that conservative, young white men feel" (Cadwalladr 2018). As Susan Brown (personal communication, June 2015) has noted, imagine what could be revealed in terms of location, class, and race through the category: buys organic bird feed.

Crucially, these algorithms perpetuate the discrimination they "find." They are not simply descriptive but also prescriptive and performative in all senses of that word. Capture systems, as Phil Agre theorized in 1994, reshape the activities they model or "discover." Through a metaphor of human activity as language, they impose a normative "grammar of action" as they move from analyzing captured data to building an epistemological model of the captured activity (364). The Chicago Police's "heat list," for instance, did not result in a reduction of homocides; it did, however, lead to subjects on the list being "2.88 times more likely than their matched counterparts to be arrested for a shooting" (Saunders, Hunt, and Hollywood 2016). It also possibly led to more homicides: those contacted by the police were afraid of being perceived as "snitches" by their neighbors (Gorner 2013). Networks create and spawn the reality they imagine; they become self-fulfilling prophecies (see Chun 2016; Healy 2015). Based on efficiency, they, like all performative systems, bypass questions of justice (see Lyotard 1984).

Performativity, however, does not simply mean the reformatting and reorganizing of the world "into line with theory" (Healy 2015, 175). Performative utterances, as Judith Butler and Jacques Derrida have argued, depend on iterability and community (Derrida 1988; Butler 1997). Butler in particular has revealed the inherent mutability of seemingly immutable and stable categories. Gender, she has argued, is performative: "it is real only to the extent that it is performed" (Butler 1988, 527). What we understand to be "natural" or "essential" is actually "manufactured through a sustained set of acts, positioned through the gendered stylization of the body . . . what we take to be an 'internal' feature of ourselves is one that we anticipate and produce through certain bodily acts, at an extreme, an hallucinatory effect of naturalized gestures" (Butler 1990, xv). These gestures and constant actions are erased/forgotten as they congeal into a "comfortable" fixed identity. As Sara Ahmed provocatively puts it: "regulative norms function in a way as repetitive strain injuries" (Ahmed 2004, 145). This understanding of performativity adds a further dimension to analyses of network performativity, for this performativity courses through networks. As I've argued more fully in *Updating to Remain the Same* (Chun 2016), networks do not simply enact what they describe, their most basic units—nodes and ties—are also themselves the consequence of performative, habitual actions.

So: what would happen if we engaged, rather than decried, network performativity? How different could this pantomime called networks be? Crucially, to take up this challenge we must realize the expressive impact of our mute actions. If Big Data, as Antoinette Rouvroy among others have argued, devalues human language by privileging bodily actions over narratives, it does so via capture systems that, as Agre points out, translate our actions into "grammars of actions" (Rouvroy 2011). Our silent—and not so silent—actions register.

To take up this challenge, we also need to move beyond dismissing Big Data as hype and celebrating "missed" predictions as evidence of our unpredictability. The gap between prediction and actuality should not foster snide comfort, especially since random recommendations are increasingly deliberately seeded to provoke spontaneous behavior. The era of Big Data is arguably a future that we reach, if we do, asymptotically, and the fact that Big Data is hype is hardly profound: most of technology is. Further, Big Data poses fascinating computational problems (how does one analyze data that one can read in once, if at all?). The plethora of correlations it documents also raises fundamental questions about causality: If almost anything can be shown to be real (if almost any correlation can be discovered), how do we know what matters, what is true? The "pre-Big Data" example of the "Super Bowl predictor" nicely encapsulates this dilemma, for one of the best predictors of the U.S. stock market is the result of the Super Bowl: if an NFC team wins, it will likely be a bull market; if an AFC team wins, it will be a bear market (Silver 2012, 185). This example also poses the question: what does knowledge do? What is the relationship between knowledge and action? The best analogy for Big Data is the mapping of the human genome: before this mapping was actualized, it was envisioned as the Holy Grail, or the Rosetta Stone for human illness. Rather than simply resulting in the cure for cancer and so forth, it raised new awareness about the importance of epigenesis, gene interactions, disease pathways, et cetera.

It is critical that we realize that the gap between prediction and reality is the space for political action and agency. Predictions can be "self-canceling" as well as self-fulfilling (Silver 2012, 219). Like global climate change and human population models, they can point to realities and futures to be rejected. They can, through their diagnosis, render impotent the predictive power of a symptom or enable new, unforeseen, grammars. To create new expressions, however, we need to read the scripts and analyze the set we find ourselves in the midst of, that is, the laboratory of network science.

Networks: The Science of Neoliberal Connections

At the most basic level, network science captures—that is, analyzes, articulates, imposes, instrumentalizes, and elaborates—connection (see the five stages of capture, Agre 1994). It is *the study of the collection, management, analysis, interpretation, and presentation of relational data*[2] (Brandes et al. 2013, 3). Described as fundamentally interdisciplinary, it brings together physics, biology, economics, social psychology, sociology, and anthropology. Put more extremely, it merges the quantitative social sciences with the physical and computer sciences in order to bypass or eliminate the humanities and media studies, two fields also steeped in theories of representation and networks. According to the acclaimed network scientist and author Albert-László Barabási, network science obviates the need for human psychology: "In the past, if you wanted to understand what humans do and why they do it, you became a card-carrying psychologist. Today you may want to obtain a degree in computer science . . . ." This is because network science, combined with "increasingly penetrating digital technologies," places us in "an immense research laboratory that, in size, complexity, and detail, surpasses everything that science has encountered before." This lab reveals "the rhythms of life as evidence of a deeper order in human behavior, one that can be explored, predicted, and no doubt exploited" (Barabási 2010, 11). Network science unravels a vast collective nonconscious, encased within the fishbowl of digital media.[3] It is the bastard child of psychoanalysis: there are no accidents, no innocent slips of the tongue. Each action is part of a larger pattern/symptom. The goal: to answer that unanswerable question, what do (wo)men want?

Network science responds to increased global connectivity and capitalism, to "a growing public fascination with the complex 'connectedness' of modern society" (Easley and Kleinberg 2010, 11). As Duncan Watts, a pioneer in this field, explains, "if this particular period in the world's history had to be characterized in any simple way, it might be as one that is more highly, more globally, and more unexpectedly connected than at any time before it." Network science is crucial to mapping and navigating "the connected age" (Watts 2004).

Network science is a version of what Fredric Jameson once called "cognitive mapping" (Jameson 1990). It is the neoliberal cure for postmodern ills (see Chun 2016). Postmodernism, according to Jameson, submerged subjects "into a multidimensional set of radically discontinuous realities, whose frames range from the still surviving spaces of bourgeois private life all the way to the unimaginable decentering of global capital itself" (Jameson 1991, 413). Because of this, they were profoundly disoriented, unable to connect their local experience (authenticity) to global systems (truth). To resolve this situation, Jameson called for cognitive mapping, a yet imaginable form of political socialist art, which corresponded to "an imperative to grow new organs, to expand our sensorium and our body to some new, yet unimaginable, perhaps ultimately impossible, dimensions" (39). Like the cognitive mapping Jameson envisioned, network science lifts the fog of postmodernism by revealing the links between the individual to the totality in which she lives. Unlike Jameson's vision, it is hardly socialist or empowering.

Rather than enabling humans to grow new organs, it contracts the world into a map: it forces a mode of authenticity shaped to an artificially intelligent truth.

Network science reduces real-world phenomena to a series of nodes and edges, which are in turn modeled to expose the patterns governing seemingly disparate behaviors, from friendship to financial crises. This mapping depends on dramatic simplifications of real world phenomena.[4] In fact, these "discovered" relations are vast simplifications of vast simplifications, with each phase of network theory—initial abstraction/representation followed by mathematical modeling—producing its own type of abstraction. The first is "applied" and "epistemological": It suggests and explicates "for given research domains, how to abstract phenomena into networks. This includes, for example, what constitutes an individual entity or a relationship, how to conceptualize the strength of a tie, etc." (Easley and Kleinberg 2010, 2). Most simply, in this stage, one decides what is a node, what is an edge, and how they should be connected. The second is "pure" network theory, for it deals "with formalized aspects of network representations such as degree distributions, closure, communities, etc., and how they relate to each other. In such pure network science, the corresponding theories are mathematical—theories of networks" (5). In this second phase, the goal is to build a model that reproduces the abstraction produced in stage one. Whatever does so is then considered true or causal. This two-step process highlights the tightrope between empiricism and modeling that network science walks: network science models not the real world but rather the initial representation and truth is what reproduces this abstraction.

These abstract relations reveal and construct a complex relationship between the local and the global. Fundamentally, network science is nonnormative: it does not assume that aggregate behaviors stem from identical agents acting identically. It connects previously discontinuous scales—the local and global, the micro and the macro—by engaging dependencies that were previously "filtered" or controlled for. It, as the authors of the inaugural volume of *Network Science* explain, differs from other sciences in its evaluation of dependency and structure. Rather than defining the domain of variables as a simple set without a structure, it assumes "at least some variables . . . to have structure. The potentially resulting dependencies are not a nuisance but more often than not they constitute the actual research interest" (Brandes et al. 2013, 8).[5] These dependencies go beyond correlations within actor attribute variables (such as the relation between income and age) to encompass the entire set of network variables. Network variables are themselves defined in terms of pairs, which are valued according to their degree (or not) of connection (for instance, 1 for connected; 0 for not). These variables in turn affect one another: "the crucial point is that the presence of one tie may influence the presence of another. . . . While this will appear an unfamiliar point of view to some, it is merely a statement that networks may be systematically patterned. Without dependence among ties, there is no emergent network structure (Brandes et al. 2013, 10).[6] At all levels, networks are dynamic and interdependent. What matters then is understanding and creating interdependencies.

Currently, modeling these interdependencies—tying global events to individual interactions—entails the marriage of graph theory with game theory, or other agent-based modeling. Computer scientist Jon Kleinberg's collaboration with economist David Easley exemplifies this fruitful combination. In their canonical and excellent textbook, *Networks, Markets, and Crowds,* based on their class at Cornell (now a popular EdX MOOC with Eva Tardos), they explain that understanding networks requires apprehending two levels of connectedness: "connectedness at the level of structure—who is connected to whom—and . . . connectedness at the level of *behavior*—the fact that each individual's actions have implicit consequences for the outcomes of everyone in the system" (Easley and Kleinberg 2010, 4). Global concerns impact local decisions, and local effects often only manifest themselves at global scales.[7] Network science thus spans the two extremes— macro-level structure and micro-level behavior—by mapping the ways that "macroscopic effects . . . arise from an intricate pattern of localized interactions" (6). *Networks, Markets, and Crowds* explicitly draws from graph theory and game theory, showing how this combination can explain seemingly "irrational" phenomena such as information cascades.

As the turn to game theory reveals, a market-based logic permeates network science models (a theme pursued later in this series by the *Markets* book by Armin Beverungen, Philip Mirowski, Edward Nik-Khah, and Jens Schroeter). Most generally, capture systems are justified and praised as inherently more efficient and empowering (and thus more democratic) than older disciplinary or firm-based ones. Agre hypothesizes that

> the computer practitioner's practice of capture is instrumental to a process by which economic actors reduce their transaction costs and thereby help transform productive activities along a trajectory towards an increasingly detailed reliance upon (or subjection to) market relations. The result is a generalized acceleration of economic activity whose social benefits in terms of productive efficiency are clear enough but whose social costs ought to be a matter of concern. (Agre 1994, 121–22)

Most succinctly: capture systems transform all transactions into market-based ones so that computerization = liberalization. Although Agre stresses that this relation is historically contingent and itself the product of a "kind of representational crusade" (120), he nonetheless hypothesizes that this relation, which "presupposes that the entire world of productive activities can be conceptualized, *a priori,* in terms of extremely numerous episodes of exchanges among economic actors," constitutes the political economy of capture (121). The language of "costs" not only underlies Agre's own critical language, it also litters the literature on networks: from attempts to model (and thus understand) collective action and critical mass (Centola 2013) to those that map differential networking techniques of women and minorities (Ibarra 1993) to those that model social learning (DiMaggio and Garip 2012); from those that seek to identify the impact of influential or susceptible members of social networks (Aral and Walker 2012) to those that analyze the "payoffs" of social capital within immigrant networks (Ooka and Wellman 2006). As this last example reveals, this market-based logic also presumes the existence of "social capital," a concept Pierre Bourdieu tied to group membership and accreditation.[8]

In the current literature, social capital explains lingering inequality among individuals. It explains disparities in success that cannot be explained in terms of individual differences in "human capital," that is, differences in intelligence, physical appearances, and skill (Burt 2002). According to sociologist Ronald S. Burt, social capital is a "metaphor or advantage" within a society "viewed as a market in which people exchange all variety of goods and ideas in pursuit of their interests." It reveals that

> the people who do better are somehow better connected. Certain people or certain groups are connected to certain others, trusting certain others, obligated to support certain others, dependent on exchange with certain others. Holding a certain position in the structure of these exchanges can be an asset in its own right. That asset is social capital, in essence, a concept of location effects in differentiated markets. (Burt 1992, 150)

A relational form of capital, it grants advantage to those who invest in social relations. It thrives off "trust" and obligation.

Marion Fourcade and Kieran Healy have refined this notion of relational capital, arguing that this form of capital is really "über-capital," which is tied to "one's position and trajectory according to various scoring, grading, and ranking methods. . . . An example would be the use of credit scores by employers or apartment owners as an indicator of an applicant's 'trustworthiness'" (Fourcade and Healy 2016, 10).[9] Fourcade and Healy's analysis thus reveals the actuarial mechanisms that construct the "trust" that Burt assumes. The term "über" denotes "the meta-, generalized,

or transcendent, nature of this capital, largely stored in the
"cloud". . . . the term über also connotes something or someone
who is extra-ordinary, who stands above the world and others . . ."
(23). This form of capital categorizes consumers based on their
"habitus" in order to make "good matches" between products and
consumers. Crucially, the categories employed by corporations do
not explicitly reference race/gender/class, for they are based on
actions rather than inherent traits. Thus,

> everyone seems to get what they deserve. Eschewing
> stereotypes, the individualized treatment of financial
> responsibility, work performance, or personal fitness by
> various forms of predictive analytics becomes harder to
> contest politically, even though it continues to work as
> a powerful agent of symbolic and material stratification.
> In other words, Übercapital subsumes circumstance and
> social structure into behavior. (33, 38)

The emphasis—in all capture systems—is on translating and figur-
ing actions.

As the above discussions of social capital and capture imply,
network science, as currently formulated, is the science of
neoliberalism. To be clear, this is not to blame network science for
neoliberalism—or to claim that network scientists are inherently
neoliberal—but to highlight the fact that the many insights network
science currently produce are deeply intertwined with the neoliberal system they presuppose. Neoliberalism, as Wendy Brown has
argued, is based on inequality and "financialized human capital":
"When we are figured as human capital in all that we do and in very
venue," she reveals, "equality ceases to be our presumed natural
relation with one another" (Brown 2015, 179). Brown elucidates the
social impact of capture systems, with their relentless rendering
of all human actions in terms of "transactions costs," namely the
destruction of democracy through the reduction of "freedom and
autonomy to unimpeded market behavior and the meaning of
citizenship to mere enfranchisement." Crucially,

this evisceration of robust norms of democracy is accompanied by unprecedented challenges to democratization, including complex forms and novel concentrations of economic and political power, sophisticated marketing and theatricality in politics, corporately owned media, and a historically unparalleled glut of information and opinion that, again, produced an illusion of knowledge, freedom, and even participation in the face of their opposites. (179)

These unprecedented challenges enumerated by Brown are exactly the challenges that network science manages by reducing public life to "problem solving and program implementation, a casting that brackets or eliminates politics, conflict, and deliberation about common values or ends" (127). Network science, as the rest of this chapter will explain, valorizes consensus, balance, and "comfort": it validates and assumes segregation by focusing on individual "preference," rather than institutional constraints and racism.

That is, to complement Fourcade and Healy's analysis and to draw from my *Updating to Remain the Same: Habitual New Media,* we need to understand how seemingly individualized scores coincide with "older" racial and class categories. Network categorizations do not only depend on your actions but on actions of your so-called neighbors—you are constantly compared to and lumped in with others. Advertisers divide the population into types such as "rising prosperity" and then subdivide that category into others such as "city sophisticates," which in turn produces categories such as "townhouse cosmopolitans" (see ACORN, developed by CACI). Neoliberalism destroys society by proliferating neighborhoods. Networks preempt and predict by reading all singular actions as indications of larger collective habitual patterns, based not on our individual actions but rather the actions of others. Correlations, that is, are not made based solely on an individual's actions and history but rather the history and actions of others "like" him or her. Through the analytic of habits, individual actions coalesce bodies into monstrously connected chimeras. That is, if as Barabási argues, "in order to predict the future, you first need to know the past" and if information technologies have made uncovering the past far easier than before, they have done so not simply through individual surveillance but through homophily (McPherson, Smith-Lovin, and Cook 2001). Homophily is the mechanism by which individuals "stick" together, and "*wes*" emerge. It is crucial to what Sara Ahmed has diagnosed as "the cultural politics of emotion": a circulation of emotions as a form of capital.

Homophily: Laundering "Our" Past

At the heart of network science is the principle of homophily: the axiom that "similarity breeds connection" (McPherson, Smith-Lovin, and Cook 2001). Homophily structures networks by creating clusters; by doing so, it also makes networks searchable (Marsden 1988; Jackson 2008). Homophily grounds network growth and dynamics, by fostering and predicting the likelihood of ties. Homophily—now a "commonsense" concept that slips between effect and cause—assumes and creates segregation; it presumes consensus and similarity within local clusters, making segregation a default characteristic of network neighborhoods. In valorizing "voluntary" actions, even as it troubles simple notions of "peer influence" and contagion, it erases historical contingencies, institutional discrimination, and economic realities (Kandel 1978; Aral, Muchnik, and Sundaraajan 2013). It serves as an alibi for the inequality it maps, while also obviating politics: homophily (often allegedly of those discriminated against)—not racism, sexism, and inequality—becomes the source of inequality, making injustice "natural" and "ecological." It turns hate into love and transforms individuals into "neighbors" who naturally want to live together, which assumes that neighborhoods should be filled with people who are alike. If we thus manage to "love our neighbor"—once considered a difficult ethical task—it is because our neighbors are virtually ourselves. Homophily makes anomalous conflicting opinions, cross-racial relationships, and heterosexuality, among many other things.

According to Miller McPherson, Lynn Smith-Lovin, and James Cook, in their definitive review article on homophily, "the homophily principle . . . structures network ties of every type, including marriage, friendship, work, advice, support, information transfer, exchange, co-membership, and other types of relationship" (2001, 415). As a result, "people's personal networks are homogeneous with regard to many sociodemographic, behavioral, and intrapersonal characteristics." Rather than framing homophily as historically contingent, they understand it as fundamental and timeless: indeed, they start their review with quotations from Aristotle and Plato about similarity determining friendship and love (which they admit in a footnote may be misleading, since Aristotle and Plato also claimed that opposites attract—indeed, homophily renders heterosexuality anomalous—a mysterious fact to be explained). Homophily, according to McPherson et al., is the result of and factor in "human ecology" (415).

Homophily sits at the fold between network structure and individual agency. As McPherson et al. summarize the "remarkably robust" patterns of homophily across numerous and diverse studies, they also break down homophily into two types: baseline homophily ("homophily effects that are created by the demography of the potential tie pool") and inbreeding homophily ("homophily measured as explicitly over and above the opportunity set") (419). McPherson et al. also reiterate Paul F. Lazarsfeld and Robert K. Merton's influential division of homophily into "status homophily," and "value homophily":

> Status homophily includes the major sociodemographic dimensions that stratify society—ascribed characteristics like race, ethnicity, sex, or age, and acquired character-istics like religion, education, occupation, or behavior patterns. Value homophily includes the wide variety of internal states presumed to shape our orientation toward future behavior. (McPherson, Smith-Lovin, and Cook, 419)

In their review, the authors note that race and ethnicity are clearly the "biggest divide in social networks today in the United States," due both to baseline and inbreeding homophily" (420). They list the following causes of homophily: geography ("the most basic source of homophily is space," (429); family ties (431); organizational foci, occupational, family, and informal roles (80); cognitive processes (434); and selective tie dissolution (435). Remarkably missing are: racism and discrimination, at personal or institutional levels, and history. In the world of networks, love, not hate, drives segregation.

Given that the very notion of homophily emerges from studies of segregation, the "discovery" of race as a divisive factor is hardly surprising. Lazarsfeld and Merton's 1954 text, in which they coined the terms "homophily" and "heterophily" (inspired by friendship categorizations of the "savage Trobianders whose native idiom at least distinguishes friendships within one's in-group from friendships outside this social circle") analyzes friendship patterns within two towns: "Craftown, a project of some seven hundred families in New Jersey, and Hilltown, a bi-racial, low-rent project of about eight hundred families in western Pennsylvania" (Lazarfeld and Merton 1954, 18–66, 23, 21). Crucially, they do not assume homophily as a grounding principle, nor do they find homophily to be "naturally" present. Rather, documenting both homophily and heterophily, they ask: "what are the dynamic processes through which the similarity or opposition of values shape the formation, maintenance, and disruption of close friendships?" (28). Homophily in their much-cited chapter is one instance of friendship formation—and one that emerges by studying the interactions between "liberal" and "illiberal" white residents of Hilltown (27). The responses of the black residents were ignored, since all these residents were classified as "liberal." As Samantha Rosenthal has noted, the very concept of value homophily is thus enfolded within status homophily (personal correspondance). Value and status are not separate—and value increasingly is used as a "code word" for race- and class-based distinctions. The implications of this segregation have been profound for the further development of network principles, as well as U.S. housing policy.

This history has been erased in the current form of network
science, in which homophily has moved problem to solution.
In the move from "representation" to "model," homophily is no
longer something to be accounted for, but rather something that
"naturally" accounts for and justifies persistence of inequality
within facially equal systems. It has become axiomatic, that is,
common sense, thus limiting the scope and possibility of network
science.[10] As Easley and Kleinberg—again two of the most insightful
and important scholars working in the field—explain: "one of the
most basic notions governing the structure of social networks is
homophily—the principle that we tend to be similar to our friends."
To make this point, they point to the distribution of "our" friends.
"Typically," they write,

> your friends don't look like a random sample of the un-
> derlying population. Viewed collectively, your friends are
> generally similar to you along racial and ethnic dimen-
> sions: they are similar in age; and they are also similar in
> characteristics that are more or less mutable, including
> the places they live, their occupations, their interests, be-
> liefs, and opinions. Clearly most of us have specific friend-
> ships that cross all these boundaries; but in aggregate,
> the pervasive fact is that links in a social network tend to
> connect people who are similar to one another. (Easley
> and Kleinberg, 78)

Homophily is a "pervasive fact" that governs the structure of
networks. As a form of natural governance—based on presump-
tions about "comfort"—it grounds network models, which not
surprisingly also "discover" segregation.[11] Like many other texts,
Damon Centola et al.'s analysis in "Homophily, Cultural Drift, and
the Co-Evolution of Cultural groups," lists "comfort" as one of
the reasons "why homophily is such a powerful force in cultural
dynamics." Referencing the work of Lazarsfeld and Merton, Centola
states: "Psychologically, we often feel justified in our feel more
comfortable opinions when we are surrounded by others who
share the same beliefs—what Lazarsfeld and Merton (1954) call

"value homophily" . . . we also feel more comfortable when we interact with others who share a similar background (i.e., status homophily)" (Centola et al. 2007, 906). To model the effects of cultural drift—and thus to show why globalization does not/will not impose a monoculture—the authors make the following assumption:

> in our approach to studying cultural dynamics, if cultural influence processes create differentiation between two neighbors such that they have no cultural traits in common, we allow these individuals to alter the structure of the social network by dropping their tie and forming new ties to other individuals. Thus, in our specification of homophily, the network of social interactions is not fixed . . . but rather evolves in tandem with the actions of the individuals. (908)

Embedded, then, in the very dynamics of network science is the presumption that there can be no neighbors without common cultural traits. Remarkably, this assumption uses Lazarsfeld and Merton's work—which, as noted earlier, did not find homophily to be "natural"—to ground their model's dynamics. Not surprisingly, Centola et al. "discover" that homophily creates "cultural niches" (926). Homophily, in so many ways, "governs" networks structure.

The point is this: although many authors such as Easley and Kleinberg insist that homophily "is often not an end point in itself but rather the starting point for deeper questions—questions that address why the homophily is present, how its underlying mechanisms will affect the further evolution of the network, and how these mechanisms interact with possible outside attempts to influence the behavior of people in the network" (83), homophily as a starting point cooks the ending point it discovers. Not only does it limit the databases used for models—these studies often draw from the same database, such as the National Longitutindal Study of Adolescent Health (ADD Health) or Facebook or Myspace, since these studies already include "friend" as a category—homophily also accentuates the clusters network science "discovers." In particular, homophily both accounts for and accentuates "triadic closure," another fundamental and "intuitive" principle of networks, which posits that "if two people in a social network have a friend in common, then there is an increased likelihood they will become friends themselves at some point in the future" (44) Although sometimes considered as a "structural" cause outside of homophily, it also presumes homophilous harmony and consensus. The reasons often given for this "very natural" phenomena are: opportunity (if A spends time with both B and C, then there is an increased chance that they will become friends), trust, and incentive ("if A is friends with B and C, then it becomes a source of latent stress in these relationship if B and C are not friends with each other" [45]). Network science posits nonconnection as unsustainable—a cause of stress. Conflict as a tie is difficult to conceive. Crucially, social networks such as Facebook (again the model organism for network science) amplify the effects of "triadic closure" and "social balance." By revealing the friends of friends—and by insisting that friendship be reciprocal—it makes triadic closure part of its algorithm: it is not simply predicted, it is predicative. As Andreas Wimmer and Kevin Lewis point out in "Beyond and Below Racial Homophily: ERG Models of a Friendship Network Documented on Facebook," Facebook's demands for reciprocity produces homophilous effects (Wimmer and Lewis 2010).

Again, homophily not only erases conflict, it also naturalizes discrimination. Segregation is what's "recovered" and justified if homophily is assumed. Easley and Kleinberg state quite simply that "one of the most readily perceived effects of homophily is the formation of ethnically and racially homogeneous neighborhoods in cities" (96). To explain this, they turn to the "Schelling model" of segregation, a simulation that maps the movement of "two distinct types of agents" in a grid. The grounding constraint is the desire of each agent "to have at least some other agents of its own as type of neighbors" (97). Showing results for this simulation, they note that spatial segregation happens even when no individual agent seeks it: the example for t = 4 (therefore, each agent would be happy as a minority) yields overwhelmingly segregated results. In response, they write:

> Segregation does not happen because it has been subtly built into the model: agents are willing to be in the minority, and they could all be satisfied if only we were able to carefully arrange them in an integrated pattern. The problem is that, from a random start, it is very hard for the collection of agents to find such integrated patterns. . . . In the long run, the process tends to cause segregated regions to grow at the expense of more integrated ones. The overall effect is one in which the local preferences of individual agents have produced a global pattern that none of them necessarily intended.
>
> This point is ultimate at the heart of the model: although segregation in real life is amplified by a genuine desire within some fraction of the population to belong to large clusters of similar people—either to avoid people who belong to other groups, or to acquire a critical mass of members from one's own group—such factors are not necessary for segregation to occur. The underpinnings of segregation are already present in a system where individuals simply want to avoid being in too extreme a minority in their own local area. (101)

I cite this at length because this interpretation reveals the dangers of homophily. The long history and legacy of race-based slavery within the United States is completely erased, as well as the importance of desegregation to the civil rights movement. There are no random initial conditions. The "initial conditions" found within the United States and the very grounding presumption that agents have a preference regarding the number of "alike" neighbors are problematic. This desire not to be in a minority—and to move if one is—maps most accurately the situations of white flight, a response to desegregation. Further, if taken as an explanation for gentrification, it portrays the movement of minorities to more affordable and less desirable areas as voluntary, rather than as the result of rising rents and taxes. Most importantly, if it finds that institutions are not to blame for segregation, it is because institutional actions are rendered invisible in these models.

Thomas C. Schelling's original publication makes this deliberate erasure of institutions and economics, as well as its engagement with white flight (or "neighborhood tipping"), clear. His now classic "Dynamic Models of Segregation" was published in 1971, during the heart of the civil rights movement and at the beginning of forced school desegregation.[12] Schelling, in his paper, acknowledges that he is deliberately excluding two main processes of segregation: organized action (it thus does not even mention the history of slavery and legally enforced segregation) and economic segregation, even though "economic segregation might statistically explain some initial degree of segregation" (145). Economic assumptions, however, are embedded at all levels in his model. Deliberate analogies to both economics and evolution ground his analysis of the "surprising results" of unorganized individual behavior.[13] He uses economic language to explain what he openly terms "discriminatory behavior."[14] At the heart of his model lies immutable difference: "I assume," he asserts,

> a population exhaustively divided into two groups; everyone's membership is permanent and recognizable. Everybody is assumed to care about the color of the people he lives among and able to observe the number of blacks and whites that occupy apiece of territory. Everybody has a particular location at any moment; and everybody is capable of moving if he is dissatisfied with the color mixture where he is. The numbers of blacks and whites, their color preferences, and the sizes of 'neighborhoods' will be manipulated. (149)

These assumptions are troubling and loaded. They erase the history of redlining and other government sanctioned programs that made it almost impossible for black citizens to buy homes in certain neighborhoods, while helping white citizens buy homes in new developments (Rothstein 2017). They also cover over the oftentimes troubling fluidity of racial identity within the United States, in particular the "one drop rule," which grounded segregation and effectively made black and white identity *not* about visible differences. As well, homophily maps hate as love. How do you show you love the same? By running away when others show up.

The erasure of history and qualitative theories about race, gender, and sexuality within social network models represents and reproduces troubling assumptions that many, within the humanities especially (but not only: think here of the overwhelming notion of the United States as "postracial" during the beginning of the Obama presidency) had thought were history. Judith Butler's definitive analysis of gender performativity at the end of the last century, combined with work in queer theory and trans studies, has made gender mutability a default assumption. The critique of race as socially constructed, which gained widespread acceptance after the horrors of the Holocaust, have been buttressed by careful historical, empirical, and theoretical studies: from Michael Omi and Howard Winant's canonical *Racial Formation in the United States* (1994) to Alondra Nelson's analysis of the genetics and race in the *Social Life of DNA: Race, Reparations, and Reconciliation after the Genome* (2016), from Paul Gilroy's controversial and provocative *Against Race: Imagining Political Culture beyond the Color Line* (2000) to Grace Elizabeth Hale's thorough examination of the Southern myth of absolute racial difference in *Making Whiteness: The Culture of Segregation in the South, 1890–1940* (1998).

Combined with so many more works, these texts document the rise of the modern concept of race during the era of Enlightenment; its centrality to colonization and slavery; its seeming zenith during the era of eugenics; its transformations after World War II; and its resurgence as an "invisible" marker in genetics. All of this is ignored within network science, when "race," "gender," and other differences are solidified as node characteristics. All of this drives twenty-first century echo chambers and politics. So what to do?

Co-relation not Correlation

Crucially, simply insisting on the fluidity of racial categories or "deconstructing" assumptions is not enough. Some work in network science does question assumptions behind racial homophily. As mentioned previously, Andreas Wimmer and Kevin Lewis have revealed that effects, understood as caused by "racial homophily," are usually caused by other factors: from homophily among coethnic groups rather than racial groups (so, underlying "Asian" homophily are tendencies of South Asians to befriend South Asians; Chinese other Chinese, et cetera) to homophily based on "socioeconomic status, regional background, and shared cultural taste" (143), to the "balancing mechanisms" employed by social media sites. (Importantly, this study was based on an extensive analysis of Facebook pages of an entire college cohort of 1,640 students.) Although this work in intersectionality is important, it is not enough, especially since intersectionality, as mentioned earlier, is exactly what "proxy factors" target, and also because this work still assumes homophily, but at different "ethnic" levels.

To create a different world, we need to question default assumptions about homophily. As Sara Ahmed has argued in *The Cultural Politics of Emotion,* "love of the same" is never innocent: white supremacist love, for instance, is based on a hatred of others (Ahmed 2004). The movement away from others, which grounds models of homophily, reveals the extent to which hatred precedes homophily. The hatred that networks foster, then, should surprise no one. Hatred, Ahmed stresses, organizes bodies. It is an emotional "investment" that makes certain bodies responsible for pain or injury. It organizes by bringing things and bodies together—by linking certain figures together so they become a common threat, an X to "our" O. Hate transforms the particular into the general: it transforms individuals into types so they become a common threat (I hate you because you are Y). It also transforms *I*s into *we*s who are threatened by this other. Homophily is never innocent: the very construction of Xs and Os, who define their discomfort in relation to the presence of others, reveals hatred, not love. Hatred is what makes possible strong bonds that define a core against a periphery. Thus, it is not only that network science seemingly makes the modeling of conflict impossible, it does so while also hiding conflict as friendship.

What this makes clear is the following: rather than mutual ignorance, apathy, or revulsion, what is needed is engagement, discussion, and yes, even conflict, in order to imagine and perform a different future. The proliferation of echo chambers and the erasure of politics is not inevitable—we can make them self-canceling prophecies. Although this will entail more than different network algorithms, these algorithms are a good place to start. What if we heeded Safiya Noble's analysis of how Google searches spread sexism and racism, and her call for better, public search engines (2018)? What if we took up Joanne Sison and Warren Sack's challenge to build democratic search engines, that is, search engines that gave users the most diverse rather than the most popular results)? How would this challenge assumptions about the "power law" (rich get richer; poor get poorer), which these algorithms foster, as well as discover? What would happen if ties did not represent friendship but rather conflict? What other world would emerge if clusters represented difference rather than similarities? What other ways would be revealed of navigating the world and of making recommendations?

Vi Hart, in her remarkable remodeling of Schelling—*The Parable of the Polygons* (2017)—makes explicit the relationship between initial conditions and history. Further, her model takes the desire for desegregation, rather than segregation, as the default. The lessons learned are thus:

1. Small individual bias ⟶ Large collective bias.
   When someone says a culture is shapist, they're not saying the individuals in it are shapist. They're not attacking you personally.

2. The past haunts the present.
   Your bedroom floor doesn't stop being dirty just coz
   you stopped dropping food all over the carpet. Creating
   equality is like staying clean: it takes work. And it's always a work in progress.

3. Demand diversity near you.
   If small biases created the mess we're in, small anti-
   biases might fix it. Look around you. Your friends, your
   colleagues, that conference you're attending. If you're
   all triangles, you're missing out on some amazing
   squares in your life—that's unfair to everyone. Reach
   out, beyond your immediate neighbors. (Hart and
   Case 2017)

Fox Harrell, a pioneer in computational media studies, also offers
a different way to engage computational modeling. Fox Harrell's
work asks: how can A.I. generate new and more humane interactions? In contrast to most computational identity systems that
incorrectly *reify* identity categories by implementing them as simple
data fields (e.g., selecting gender from a brief drop-down menu)
or a collection of attributes (e.g., races represented as modifiers
to numerical statistics and constrained graphical characteristics
in computer games), he has developed the AIR (Advanced Identity
Representation) project to produce "computational models of
subjective identity phenomena related to categorization such as
specific forms of marginalization that are overlooked in engineering" (Harrell 2013, 1). Crucially, systems he has built, such
as *Chimeria: Gatekeeper,* confront users with the fluidity of racial
identifications and the difficulties of managing discrimination
based on stereotypes and the limitations of passing. Further, his
analyses of existing systems and user interactions with his systems
based on "archetypal analyses," exposes and analyzes the "ideal
players" embedded within popular games and how they can perpetuate stereotypes through the actions they enable and prohibit.
For instance, he reveals how certain "species" within games line up

with certain stereotypical assumptions about races, as well as how user actions with differently gendered avatars reveal assumptions about gender.

Harrell's work most critically engages the creativity embedded within artificial intelligence. *Phantasmal Media: An Approach to Imagination, Computation, and Expression* (2013), drawn from his work with Define Me and GRIOT, groundbreaking social networking and expressive A.I. projects, asks: can A.I. have the same impact as great literature, such as Ralph Ellison's *Invisible Man*? That is, through its powerful imagery and literary innovations, can A.I. enable its readers to experience the world of social invisibility? Can A.I. imagine different, more just worlds, while also exposing the extent to which society and ideology are linked to the imagination? To produce computational and interactive narratives that do this, Harrell in his first book developed a theory of phantasmal media, in which a phantasm is a combination of imagery and ideas. By focusing on the role of phantasms, Harrell addresses not simply the centrality of the imagination to individual experience but also the relationship between individuals and larger cultural and political issues. Significantly, Harrell does not simply condemn phantasms as unreal and unjust but rather reveals how they can be both empowering and oppressive. They are forms of agency play. Through a comparative analysis that reveals the experiences of those normally excluded from mainstream society, his work thus both exposes the negative impact of phantasms and produces new phantasms that allow his users to imagine new worlds. That is, his work in cultural computing makes visible cultural phantasms in order to diversify the range and impact of computing systems. For instance, by revealing the cultural phantasms behind notions of grey/black sheep (persons who do not fit nicely into preconceived identity and behavioral categorizations), Harrell transforms them from errors into rich sources of knowledge. As well (and as noted earlier), critical computing enables empowerment and agency, where agency is not the freedom to do anything one wants but rather the situated mechanisms for user action within the context

of cultural phantasms. By thinking expressive, cultural, and critical
computing together, Harrell shows how embodied individual
experiences are created and how the social and the computational
are linked together through the phantasmal.

As well as this new type of artificial intelligence, new theories of
connection—which do not presume a dangerously banal and
reciprocal notion of friendship—are needed. Rather than similarity
as breeding connection, we need to think, with Ahmed, through
the generative power of discomfort. We need to queer homophily,
a concept that should in its very nature be queer. Ahmed views
queerness as an inability to be comfortable in certain norms:

> To feel uncomfortable is precisely to be affected by that
> which persists in the shaping of bodies and lives. Discom-
> fort is hence not about assimilation or resistance, *but
> about inhabiting norms differently.* The inhabitance is gen-
> erative or productive insofar as it does not end with the
> failure of norms to be secured, but with the possibilities
> of living that do not "follow" those norms through. (em-
> phasis in original, 155).

To be uncomfortable, then, is to inhabit norms differently, to create
new ways of living with others—different ways of impressing upon
others. Working with Ahmed and others, we can imagine new
defaults, new forms of engagement. Different, more inhabitable,
patterns.

We also need to examine theoretical moves and assumptions
within the humanities. That the humanities and cultural theory
more generally have moved away from questions of cultural difference and identity at a time when such an engagement could not
be more crucial is mind-boggling. The various turns toward "less
coarse" and "static" concepts such as nonhuman allure (themselves
inspired by networks and new media), not to mention the embrace
of an instrumentalist technological logic that demeans critical
analysis and celebrates digital tinkering, are oddly contradictory
and self-defeating. The early twenty-first century has witnessed a

move away from theories of performativity, mutability, and deep interpretation, just when such theories are crucial to unpacking, re-imagining and remaking the retrograde identity politics embedded within the world of networks. By refusing to analyze and engage these patterns—by refusing to use the "old" keys in our pocket—we lock ourselves into a future we allegedly oppose.

The future lies in the new patterns we can create together, new forms of relation that include liveable forms of indifference. The future lies in unusual collaborations that both respect and challenge methods and insights, across disciplines and institutions.

Notes

1   For an overview, see Sweeney and Haney 1992. During this same period, this was made clear in the disparity between jail sentences given to two U.S. male college athletes for sexually assaulting unconscious women. Corey Batey, a nineteen-year-old African American football player at Vanderbilt was sentenced to a mandatory minimum sentence of fifteen to twenty-five years; Brock Turner, a nineteen-year-old swimmer at Stanford was sentenced to six months, which could be shortened for good behavior (see King 2016).

2   These editors of *Network Science* made the following claims in their introduction to the inaugural issue:

   Claim 1: Network science is the study of network models.
   Claim 2: There are theories about network representations and network theories about phenomena: both constitute network theory.
   Claim 3: Network science should be empirical—not exclusively so, but consistently—and its value assessed against alternative representations.
   Claim 4: What sets network data apart is the incidence structure of its domain.
   Claim 5: At the heart of network science is dependence, both between and within variables.
   Claim 6: Network science is evolving into a mathematical science in its own right.
   Claim 7: Network science is itself more of an evolving network than a paradigm expanding from a big bang. (Brandes et al. 2013, 1–15)

3   Barabási's description resonates with cyberpunk fiction, which posits artificial intelligence and supreme cowboy hackers as capable of detecting "patterns . . . in the dance of the street" and thus foresee events that elude mere humans (see Gibson 1984, 250).

4   As Duncan Watts notes: "The truth is that most of the actual science here com-

prises extremely simple representations of extremely complicated phenomena. Starting off simple is an essential stage of understanding anything complex, and the results derived from simple models are often not only powerful but also deeply fascinating. By stripping away the confounding details of a complicated world, by searching for the core of a problem, we can often learn things about connected systems that we would never guess from studying them directly. The cost is that the methods we use are often abstract, and the results are hard to apply directly to real applications. It is a necessary cost, unavoidable in fact, if we truly desire to make progress" (Watts 2004).

5   The example they give of the difference between network science and statistic is quite illuminating: "While the range of attributes is structured, in much of science, the domain on which variables are defined is assumed to have no structure, i.e., simply a set. This may be for good reason. If we are interested in associations between, say, education and income controlled for age, we actually do not want there to be relations between individuals that also moderate the association. Much of statistics is in fact concerned with detecting and eliminating such relations. Network science, on the other hand, seeks to understand the correspondence and impact of these relations, rather than control for any variable" (Brandes et al. 2013, 8).

6   As Easley and Kleinberg explain, "the pattern of connections in a given system can be represented as a network, the components of the system being the network vertices and the connections the edges. Upon reflection it should come as no surprise (although in some fields it is a relatively recent realization) that the structure of such networks, the particular pattern of interactions, can have a big effect on the behavior of a system. . . . A network is a simplified representation that reduces a system to an abstract structure capturing only the basics of connection patterns and little else (Easley and Kleinberg 2010, 2).

7   They write: "in a network setting, you should evaluate your actions not in isolation but with the expectation that the world will react to what you do." This makes "cause-and-effect relationships . . . quite subtle" and may only become evident at the population level" (Easley and Kleinberg 2010, 5).

8   Pierre Bourdieu defined social capital as: "the aggregate of the actual or potential resources which are linked to possession of a durable network of more or less institutionalized relationships of mutual acquaintance and recognition—or in other words, to membership in a group" (Bourdieu 1986). Social capital is a form of credit or credentialing that relies on reciprocal and networked acknowledgement and exchange. This form of capital, he stresses, exists "only in the practical state, in material and/or symbolic exchanges which help to maintain them." The ties, that is, are dynamic and constantly enacted.

9   As Cramer writes: "The reduction of audience members to countable numbers—data sets, indices—is thus a self-fulfilling prophecy of stability" (Cramer in this volume).

10   By 1977, homophily was already accepted as an axiomatic if problematic aspect of society. In an equally key early text, *Inequality and Heterogeneity: A Primitive Theory of Social Structure,* Peter Blau outlined what would become "contact

theory": the theory that contact creates integration. An ambitious attempt to create a roadmap of "macrosociological theory" (written in the spirit of Karl Marx and Georg Simmel), it argued for the importance of "weak ties" and heterogeneity to combat inequality within society. As he put it, heterogeneity and inequality were "complementary opposites" and "there can be too much inequality, but cannot be too much heterogeneity" (Blau 1977, 11). Blau argued strongly for the replacement of "strong ingroup bonds," which "restrain individual freedom and mobility . . . and sustain rigidity and bigotry" with "diverse intergroup relations" (85). These heterogeneous relations, "though not intimate, foster tolerance, improve opportunities, and are essential for the integration of a large society" (85). In terms that resonated with Jameson's description of postmodernism and the possibilities of "cognitive mapping," he states, "the loss of extensive strong bonds in a community of kin and neighbors undoubtedly has robbed individuals of a deep sense of belonging and having roots, of profound feelings of security and lack of anxiety. This is the price we pay for the greater tolerance and opportunities that distinguish modern societies, with all their grievous faults, from primitive tribes and feudal orders. The social integration of individuals in modern society rests no longer exclusively on strong bonds with particular ingroups but in good part on multiple supports from wider networks of weaker social ties, supplemented by a few intimate bonds" (85). This insight itself draws from the work of another early progenitor of network science, Mark Granovetter's 1973 theorization of "weak ties" as essential to information dissemination and success. For more on this in relation to networks as dissolving postmodern confusion, see Chun (2016). Tellingly, Blau's argument assumes—and indeed takes as axiomatic—the fact that ingroup interactions are greater than intergroup ones (Axiom A1.1). It also divides and identifies individuals based on structural parameters, such as "age, race, education, and socioeconomic status," some of which Blau considers "inborn" (1977, 6).

11 For instance, Lenore Newman and Ann Dalez state: "We feel more comfortable with those like ourselves, even in virtual communities." (2007, 79–90).

12 In 1972, the NAACP filed a class action lawsuit against the Boston School Committee—Bostong is contiguous with Cambridge, Massachusetts, which is where Harvard is located.

13 Schelling writes: "economists are familiar with systems that lead to aggregate results that the individual neither intends nor needs to be aware of, results that sometimes have no recognizable counterpart at the level of the individual. The creation of money by a commercial banking system is one; the way savings decisions cause depressions or inflations is another. Similarly, biological evolution is responsible for a lot of sorting and separating, but the little creatures that mate and reproduce and forage for food would be amazed to know that they were bringing about separation of species, territorial sorting, or the extinction of species" (Schelling 1971, 145). Schelling also uses the term "incentives" to explain segregation: from preferences to avoidance to economic constraints (148).

14   At the start of this article, Schelling explains: "This article is about the kinds of
     segregation—or separation, or sorting—that can result from discriminatory
     individual behavior. By 'discriminatory,' I mean reflecting an awareness, con-
     scious or unconscious, of sex or age or religion or color or whatever the basis
     of segregation is, an awareness that influences decisions on where to live,
     whom to sit by, what occupation to join or avoid, whom to play with or whom
     to talk to" (144).

References

ACORN. 2013. "What Is ACORN?" *Caci.* Accessed March 1, 2016. http://acorn.caci.co.uk.

Agre, Phil. 1994. "Surveillance and Capture: Two Models of Privacy." *The Information Society* 100: 101–27.

Ahmed, Sara. 2004. *The Cultural Politics of Emotion.* London: Routledge.

Al Zamal, Faiyaz, Wendy Liu, and Derek Ruths. 2012. "Homophily and Latent Attribute Inference: Inferring Latent Attributes of Twitter Users from Neighbors." *Proceedings of the Sixth International AAAI Conference on Weblogs and Social Media.* https://www.aaai.org/ocs/index.php/ICWSM/ICWSM12/paper/viewFile/4713/5013.

Angwin, Julio, Jeff Larson, Surya Mattu, and Lauren Kirchner. 2016. "Machine Bias: There's Software Used Across the Country to Predict Future Criminals. And It's Biased against Blacks." *ProPublica.* Accessed May 23, 2016. https://www.propublica.org/article/machine-bias-risk-assessments-in-criminal-sentencing.

Aral, Sinan, and Dylan Walker. 2012. "Identifying Influential and Susceptible Members of Social Networks." *Science* 337: 337–41.

Aral, Sinan, Lev Muchnik, and Arun Sundaraajan. 2013. "Engineering Social Contagions: Optimal Network Seeding and Incentive Strategies." *Network Science* 1, no. 2: 125–53.

Barabási, Albert-László. 2010. *Bursts: The Hidden Patters behind Everything We Do, from Your E-mail to Bloody Crusades.* New York: Plume.

Bernstein, Elizabeth. 2007. *Temporarily Yours: Intimacy, Authenticity, and the Commerce of Sex.* Chicago: University of Chicago.

Blarr, Alistair. 2015. "Google Mistakenly Tags Black People as 'Gorillas,' Showing Limits of Algorithms." *The Wall Street Journal.* Accessed July 1, 2015. http://blogs.wsj.com/digits/2015/07/01/google-mistakenly-tags-black-people-as-gorillas-showing-limits-of-algorithms/.

Blau, Peter M. 1977. *Inequality and Heterogeneity: A Primitive Theory of Social Structure.* New York: The Free Press.

Bourdieu, Pierre. 1986. "The Forms of Capital." In *Handbook of Theory and Research for the Sociology of Education,* edited by John G. Richardson, 241–58. New York: Greenwood.

Brandes, Ulrik, et al. 2013. "What Is Network Science?" *Network Science* 1, no. 1: 1–15.

Brown, Wendy. 2015. *Undoing the Demos: Neoliberalism's Stealth Revolution.* Cambridge, Mass.: MIT Press.

Burt, Ronald S. 2002. "Chapter 7: The Social Capital of Structural Holes." In *The New*

Economic Sociology: Developments in an Emerging Field, edited by Marshall Meyer, Maruo F. Guillen, Randall Collins, and Paula England, 148–92. New York: Russell Sage.

Burt, Ronald S. 1992. *Structural Holes: The Social Structure of Competition.* Cambridge, Mass.: Harvard University Press.

Butler, Judith. 1988. "Performative Acts and Gender Constitution: An Essay in Phenomenology and Feminist Theory." *Theater Journal* 40, no. 4: 519–31.

Butler, Judith. 1990. *Gender Trouble: Feminism and the Subversion of Identity.* London: Routledge.

Butler, Judith. 1997. *Excitable Speech: A Politics of the Performative.* London: Routledge.

Cadwalladr, Carole. 2018. "'I Made Steve Bannon's Psychological Warfare Tool': Meet the Data War Whistleblower," *The Guardian.* Accessed July 5, 2018. https://www.theguardian.com/news/2018/mar/17/data-war-whistleblower-christopher-wylie-faceook-nix-bannon-trump.

Centola, Damon M. 2013. "Homophily, Networks, and Critical Mass: Solving the Start-up Problem in Large Group Collective Action." *Rationality and Society* 15 (1): 3–40.

Centola, Damon, Juan Carlos González-Avella, Víctor M. Eguíluz, and Maxi San Miguel. 2007. "Homophily, Cultural Drift, and the CO-Evolution of Cultural Groups." *The Journal of Conflict Resolution* 51, no. 6: 905–29.

Chun, Wendy Hui Kyong. 2016. *Updating to Remain the Same: Habitual New Media.* Cambridge, Mass.: MIT Press.

Crawford, Kim, and Jason Schultz. 2014. "Big Data and Due Process: Toward a Framework to Redress Predictive Privacy Harms." *Boston College Law Review* 55, no. 1: 93–128. http://lawdigitalcommons.bc.edu/cgi/viewcontent.cgi?article=3351&context=bclr.

Crenshaw, Kimberlé. 1991. "Mapping the Margins: Intersectionality, Identity Politics, and Violence against Women of Color." *Stanford Law Review* 43, no. 6: 1241–99.

Derrida, Jacques. 1988. "Signature, Event, Context." In *Limited Inc.,* translated by Samuel Weber, 1–23. Evanston, Ill.: Northwestern University Press.

DiMaggio, Paul, and Filiz Garip. 2012. "Network Effects and Social Inequality." *Annual Review of Sociology* 38:93–118.

Dyer, Richard. 1997. *White: Essays on Race and Culture.* London: Routledge.

Easley, David, and Jon Kleinberg. 2010. *Networks, Crowds, and Markets: Reasoning about a Highly Connected World.* Cambridge: Cambridge University Press.

Fourcade, Marion, and Kieran Healy. 2016. "Seeing Like a Market." *Socio-Economic Review* 15, no. 1: 1–21.

Frucci, Adam. 2009. "HP Face-Tracking Webcams Don't Recognize Black People." *Gizmodo.* Accessed December 21, 2009. http://gizmodo.com/5431190/hp-face-tracking-webcams-dont-recognize-black-people.

Gibson, William. 1984. *Neuromancer.* New York: ACE.

Gilroy, Paul. 2000. *Against Race: Imagining Political Culture beyond the Color Line.* Cambridge, Mass.: Harvard University Press.

Gorner, Jeremy. 2013. "Chicago Police Use 'Heat List' as Strategy to Prevent Violence." *The Chicago Tribune.* Accessed August 21, 2013. http://articles.chicagotribune

.com/2013–08–21/news/ct-met-heat-list-20130821_1_chicago-police-commander
-andrew-papachristos-heat-list.

Granovetter, Mark. 1973. "The Strength of Weak Ties." *American Journal of Sociology* 78, no. 6: 1360–80.

Hale, Grace Elizabeth. 1998. *Making Whiteness: The Culture of Segregation in the South, 1890–1940.* New York: Pantheon Books.

Harrell, D. Fox. 2013. *Phantasmal Media: An Approach to Imagination, Computation, and Expression.* Cambridge, Mass.: MIT Press.

Harris, Meena. 2016. "Talking with Black Women Engineers about Diversity in Silicon Valley." *Lenny.* Accessed March 1, 2016. http://www.lennyletter.com/work/a283/ talking-with-black-women-engineers-about-diversity-in-silicon-valley/.

Hart, Vi, and Nick Case. 2017. "Parable of the Polygons." Accessed June 29, 2017. http://ncase.me/polygons/

Healy, Kieran. 2015. "The Performativity of Networks." *European Journal of Sociology* 52, no. 2: 175–205.

Ibarra, Herminia. 1993. "Personal Networks of Women and Minorities in Manage-ment: A Conceptual Framework." *The Academy of Management Review* 18, no. 1: 56–87.

Ingram, Matthew. 2016. "Why Getting Rid of Human Editors Won't Solve Facebook's Bias Problem." *Fortune.* Accessed August 29, 2016. http://fortune.com/2016/08/29/ facebook-trending-human-bias/.

Jackson, Matthew O. 2008. "Average Distance, Diameter, and Clustering in Social Net-works with Homophily." In *Internet and Network Economics: Proceedings of the 4th International Workshop WINE 2008,* edited by Christos Papdimitriou and Shuzhong Zhang, 4–11. Berlin: Springer-Verlag.

Jameson, Frederic. 1990. "Cognitive Mapping." In *Marxism and the Interpretation of Culture,* edited by Cary Nelson and Lawrence Grossberg, 347–60. Urbana and Chicago: University of Illinois Press.

Jameson, Frederic. 1991. *Postmodernism, or the Cultural Logic of Late Capitalism.* London: Verso.

Kandel, Denise B. 1978. "Homophily, Selection, and Socialization in Adolescent Friendships." *American Journal of Sociology* 84, no. 2: 427–36.

King, Shawn. 2016. "Brock Turner and Cory Batey, Two College Athletes Who Raped Unconscious Women, Show How Race and Privilege Affect Sentences." *New York Daily News.* Accessed June 7, 2016. http://www.nydailynews.com/news/ national/king-brock-turner-cory-batey-show-race-affects-sentencing-article-1 .2664945.

Lartey, Jamiles. 2016. "Predictive Policing Practices Labeled as 'Flawed' by Civil Rights Coalition." *The Guardian.* Accessed August 31, 2016. https://www.theguardian .com/us-news/2016/aug/31/predictive-policing-civil-rights-coalition-aclu.

Lazarsfeld, Paul F., and Robert K. Merton. 1954. "Friendship as Social Process: A Sub-stantive and Methodological Analysis." In *Freedom and Control in Modern Society,* edited by Morroe Berger, Theodore Abel, and Charles H. Page, 18–66. Toronto: D. Van Nostrand Company, Inc.

Lee, Odelia. 2009. "Camera Misses the Mark on Racial Sensitivity." *Gizmodo.* Accessed

May 15, 2009. http://gizmodo.com/5256650/camera-misses-the-mark-on-racial
-sensitivity.

Lyotard, Jean-François. 1984. *The Postmodern Condition: A Report on Knowledge.* Minneapolis: University of Minnesota Press.

Marsden, Peter V. 1988. "Homogeneity in Confiding Relations." *Social Networks* 10,
no. 1: 57–76.

McPherson, Miller, Lynn Smith-Lovin, and James Cook. 2001. "Birds of a Feather:
Homophily in Social Networks." *Annual Review of Sociology* 27:415–44.

Nelson, Alondra. 2016. *Social Life of DNA: Race, Reparations, and Reconciliation after the
Genome.* Boston: Beacon Press.

Newman, Lenore, and Ann Dalez. 2007. "Homophily and Agency: Creating Effective
Sustainable Development Networks." *Environment, Development, and Sustainability*
9:79–90.

Noble, Safiya Umoja. 2018. *Algorithms of Oppression: How Search Engines Reinforce
Racism.* New York: New York University Press.

Omi, Michael, and Howard Winant. 1994. *Racial Formation in the United States: From
the 1960s to the 1990s,* 2nd edition. New York: Routledge.

O'Neil, Cathy. 2016. *Weapons of Math Destruction: How Big Data Increases Inequality
and Threatens Democracy.* London: Penguin.

Ooka, Emi, and Barry Wellman. 2006. "Does Social Capital Pay Off More within or between Ethnic Groups? Analyzing Job Searches in Five Toronto Ethnic Groups." In *Inside the Mosaic,* edited by Erik Fong, 199–226. Toronto: University of Toronto Press.

Phillips, Whitney. 2015. *This Is Why We Can't Have Nice Things: Mapping the Relationship
between Online Trolling and Mainstream Culture.* Cambridge, MA: MIT Press.

Pinboard. 2016. "Machine Learning Is Money Laundering for Bias." Accessed August
29, 2016. https://twitter.com/pinboard/status/744595961217835008.

Robinson, David, and Logan Koepke. 2016. "Stuck in a Patter: Early Evidence on 'Predictive Policing' and Civil Rights." *Upturn.* Accessed August 30, 2016. https://www
.teamupturn.com/reports/2016/stuck-in-a-pattern.

Rothstein, Richard. 2017. *The Color of Law: A Forgotten History of How Our Government
Segregated America.* New York and London: Liveright Publishing Corporation, a
Division of W.W. Norton & Company.

Rouvroy, Antoinette. 2011. "Technology, Virtuality, and Utopia: Governmentality in
an Age of Autonomic Computing." In *The Philosophy of Law Meets the Philosophy of
Technology: Autonomic Computing and Transformations of Human Agency,* edited by
Mireille Hildebrandt and Antoinette Rouvroy, 136–57. Milton Park, UK: Routledge.

Saunders, Jessica, Priscilla Hunt, and John S. Hollywood. 2016. "Predictions Put into
Practice: A Quasi-Experimental Evaluation of Chicago's Predictive Policing Pilot."
Journal of Experimental Criminology 22, no. 3: 347–71. http://link.springer.com/
article/10.1007/s11292-016-9272-0.

Schelling, Thomas C. 1971. "Dynamic Models of Segregation." *Journal of Mathematical
Sociology* 1:143–86.

Silver, Nate. 2012. *The Signal and the Noise: Why So Many Predictions Fail—but Some
Don't.* New York: Penguin Books.

Sweeney, Laura T., and Craig Haney. 1992. "The Influence of Race on Sentencing: A

Meta-Analytic Review of Experimental Studies." *Behavioral Sciences and the Law* 10, no. 2: 179–95.

Thielman, Sam. 2016. "Facebook Fires Trending Team, and Algorithm without Humans Goes Crazy." *The Guardian.* Accessed August 29, 2016. https://www.theguardian .com/technology/2016/aug/29/facebook-fires-trending-topics-team-algorithm.

Watts, Duncan J. 2004. *Six Degrees: The Science of a Connected Age* (Kindle Locations 191–94). W. W. Norton. Kindle Edition.

Wimmer, Andreas, and Kevin Lewis. 2010. "Beyond and Below Racial Homophily: ERG Models of a Friendship Network Documented on Facebook." *American Journal of Sociology* 116, no. 2: 642–83.

4

Data Paranoia: How to Make Sense of Pattern Discrimination

Clemens Apprich

When I want to communicate with another person, I have at hand
a number of old and new methods: languages, systems of writing,
means of storing, of transmitting, or of multiplying the message—
tapes, telephone, printing press, and so on.

—Michel Serres, Hermes

In Michel Serres's *Hermes* (1982) we follow the mythical journey of
the Greek god, whose goal it is to deliver a message to different
protagonists of European cultural history. During this journey the
message gets translated, transformed, and multiplied through
diverse means of communication and spaces of knowledge,
reaching from mythology to science, from philosophy to literature,
from mathematics to biology, thermodynamics, and cybernetics.
These fields constitute the nodal points of a global network of
communication, which Hermes constantly weaves into a fabric of
circular codes. Hence, the namegiver of modern *Hermeneutics* is the
divine herald of all communication. But at the same time, and this
is Serres's punchline, he is a parasite of communication, a trickster,

who subverts the symbolic order he builds in the first place. Similar to the figure of the hacker (see Pias 2002), he has to disassemble the code before he can reassemble it. Hermes, in this sense, causes disorder, interference, and confusion, the background noise against which the meaning of a message can only take shape (see Harari and Bell 1982, xxv). However, this noise must be excluded in order to maintain the illusion of frictionless communication.

According to Serres, in communication a smooth transfer is not the norm but rather the exception. Misunderstanding and divergent interpretations are an integral part of the symbolic order. So even if we misunderstand a certain situation, there is an attempt to catch its meaning. It is always a common meaning and symbolic order that our understanding is referring to. Without this common meaning there is no understanding. Understanding, therefore, necessitates an intersubjectively produced meaning; it implies a collective principle of comprehension, assuming that this principle is always about to fail. From this perspective, hermeneutics is not only the methodology of interpretation but also the general theory of understanding (see Schleiermacher 1998). It does refer to reproductive comprehension, understood as interpretation of a pregiven symbolic system, as well as productive understanding, which implies an attribution of meaning. In particular, the latter is of importance for the book at hand, because it relates to an authoritative—although not necessarily authoritarian—entity, a master signifier organizing meaning. Hence, even though—or pre-cisely because—there is no necessary analogy between reality and its symbolization, meaning is attributed to the world by a symbolic order, which, ultimately, functions as an ideological system (see Žižek 2008, 95–97).[1]

Big Data, it seems, proceeds to become a new ideology with its very own horizon of meaning. As Florian Cramer suggests in his contri-bution to this book, hermeneutics therefore has enjoyed a revival with Big Data analytics, even though it now has to be considered a "backdoor hermeneutics." In times of the so-called fourth paradigm (see Hey, Tansley, and Tolle 2009),[2] data-intensive computing yields a new form of analysis that is no longer about the interpretation of the past but rather focuses on speculating about the future. However, far from being a neutral tool for capturing, curating, and analyzing, Big Data is based on its very own interpretative framework: "Just like the Oracle of Delphi, it is dependent on interpretation" (see Cramer in this volume). And according to Cramer, this "interpretative capability is limited by algorithmics—so that the limitations of the tool (and, ultimately, of using mathematics to process meaning) end up defining the limits of interpretation." Herein lies the whole problem with data analytics analyzed in this volume: the process of understanding something *as* something—the formal structure of any understanding and thus of hermeneutics—disappears into a nirvana of algorithmic computation, which is no longer intelligible to the human mind.[3]

Yet one could ask if the disappearance of this process isn't an integral part of communication itself? At least this is Serres's point when he questions modern information theory, which, for him, is only one particular case within the problem of communication (Serres 1982, 71–83). For Serres the problem is not so much about how to encode or decode a message; that is, to know the code. Rather the problem lies in the fact that for a communicative act to be successful, the underlying code has to be hidden. This becomes apparent when we think about dominant meanings in the cultural, social, and political world, which are necessary preconditions if we want to make sense of—or even critique—everyday life (see Hall 1999). In order to be part of it, one has to speak and understand the common language, without referring to it all the time.[4] This taken-for-granted knowledge constitutes an organizational principle of understanding, a master signifier, to which both the psychic and social individual are subjected. Hence, Hermes does not simply deliver the messages of the gods, which then have to be interpreted. Being a god himself, he represents the system of symbols within which a common reality is constructed and therefore communication can take place. Hermes is messenger, translator, and authoritative figure in one. And as god of disguise, he is aware of the fact that successful communication requires his exclusion as mediator (Serres 1982, 67). Such an awareness also depicts the challenge of this book: neither does it want to repeat the pervasive belief that algorithms are just too complex to be understood, nor take the bait that by simply making every communication step transparent, the problem can be solved.

In order to filter a message out of noise, to literally discriminate data to extract information, the discriminatory patterns within the communication process have to work behind the scene. This is the hermeneutical paradox and the reason Michel Serres considers Hermes to be the patron saint of our postmodern time. As soon as Hermes enters the stage to deliver the message, he blurs and renders it unintelligible; only after he disappears does the message become legible. He is the excluded third in every communication process, like algorithms, which are present and absent at the same time. With new information and communication technologies, we live in a time of such paradoxes, often compared to the passage from oral to written culture (see Stiegler 2012) or from writing to printing (see Builder 1993). As a consequence, the cultural logic of late capitalism is entangled into a postmodern confusion (see Jameson 1991), propelled by a "decline of symbolic efficiency" (Dean 2010, 6)[5]. The symbolic order resembles a flip-flop picture: Like Hermes, it constantly changes its state, leaving us in the dark about its actual meaning. But as can be seen from Hermes's journey, pictured by Serres as a succession of random encounters and discoveries, every disconnection entails a reconnection; the interruption of a symbolic order of exchange allows for the production of a new, more complex order (see Serres 1982).

Connecting People Apart

In times of global connectedness, the symbolic order we live in gets more and more complicated. As Wendy Hui Kyong Chun argues in her piece in this volume, we have to critically engage with this order, rather than simply dismiss it as the latest hype of capitalist innovation. According to her, we need to work through the problems posed by network analytics, in particular its excessive search for correlations: "If almost anything can be shown to be real (if almost any correlation can be discovered), how do we know what matters, what is true?" In our networked environments, network analytics has become the default model, on the basis of which causality gets replaced by data correlation. We live in a flat ontology of likeness and similarity, within which every fact is correlated to another fact, with the effect that no fact is of significance anymore (see Lynch 2016). Yet this analysis is far from new; Friedrich Nietzsche already came up with the idea of a postfact world, where there are no facts but only interpretations (see Nietzsche 1989). What is new, though, is the fragmentation of largely stable knowledge sources into an atomized world of updates, comments, opinions, rumors, and gossip. In order to be able to filter information from this constant stream of data, we rely on algorithms, helping us to bring order into our new media life. In this sense, Facebook, Google, and company create a habitual environment, a seemingly personalized world, which keeps us in a state of self-identification through social segregation (see Chun 2016).

The salient point of Chun's text is the conclusion that these isolated worlds, also called echo chambers or filter bubbles, are not simply manifestations of a "natural" preference of individuals to bond with similar individuals, but have to be constantly produced and reproduced. Hence, behind the concept of homophily the "old" power relations of class, race, and gender flare up. But instead of "new theories of connections" (Chun in this volume), in order to cut through the ideological linkage of Big Data and network analytics, we are confronted with "the end of theory" (see Anderson 2008), a claim that is deeply problematic, because it tends to obfuscate what is crucially needed: a critical knowledge about the (sexist, racist, classist) mechanisms underlying today's networked sociality. This not only affects the technological aspect of pattern discrimination but also our very understanding of democracy. If data speaks for itself, an informed debate about how and for whom it works

becomes obsolete. Likewise, classical hermeneutics, in the sense
of a positive or negative interpretation of existing normative
symbols, gets replaced by free-floating cosmographies, understood as attempts to map the world without a common point
of reference.

In the digital world a new "hermeneutics of suspicion" (Ricoeur
1970, 32) vis-à-vis media technologies is necessary.[6] As Boris Groys
has argued, such a "media-ontological suspicion" isn't simply a
subjective illusion, arising in the imaginary of an individual, but
an objective phenomenon, which appears during the act of media
observation itself: "As observers of the media, we are simply
incapable of seeing anything else in the media but loci of hidden
manipulation" (Groys 2012, 38). The paranoid doubt, according to
Groys, cannot be suspended, because the submedial space—that
is, the space lurking behind the symbolic surface of media—is
structurally hidden. As is the case with the divine dis/appearance
of Hermes, "we have no choice but to suspect, to project, and to
insinuate" (38). Hence, we inevitably assume manipulation behind
the media, which remains a dark space to us; and still we build
upon the reality constituted by it. For Niklas Luhmann this is one
of the paradox effects of the functional differentiation of modern
society: "Whatever we know about our society, or indeed about the
world in which we live, we know through the mass media. . . .
On the other hand, we know so much about the mass media that
we are not able to trust these sources" (Luhmann 2000, 1). Yet
Luhmann is still assuming that there is only one reality constructed by mass media, while today, with the emergence of digital
media, we have to consider a variety of realities in different media
settings, which makes the media-ontological question even more
complicated.

Due to the diversity of media formats and offerings supported by
the internet, the "construction of reality" (Luhmann 2000, 76) has
been dispersed into a network of simultaneously existing realities.
While mass media, with its basic principles of periodicity, publicity,
universality, and topicality, has established a common public

sphere within which—at least in an idealized world—all citizens are able to participate in rational deliberation (see Habermas 1989, 244–48), the actual realization of participatory media in the form of social media has led to a fragmentation of a mass-mediated public into partial publics (see Hagen 2016). This shift from mass media to social media is accompanied by the rise of web-based communication applications, the ubiquity of mobile computing and the formation of powerful media platforms, all of which are deeply enmeshed with our everyday media life (see van Dijck and Poell 2013). According to José van Dijck and Thomas Poell, social media is characterized by four principles, which, over the past years, have gradually infiltrated the logic of mass media: programmability, popularity, connectivity, and datafication. The latter in particular can be seen as a crucial aspect of a data-driven world, because it "refers to the ability of networked platforms to render into data many aspects of the world that have never been quantified before" (9). Real-time data flows, unprecedented in their volume and constantly collected, provide the commercial basis of a whole new industry, which tries both to predict and shape the behavior of users, and, as a consequence, redefine our understanding of participation: in the interplay between how things are and how they might be (see Beyes and Pias 2016), a data-driven world becomes a malleable compound that can yield very different results.

With Big Data and social media platforms the public sphere gets more and more fragmented (see Varnelis 2008).[7] For instance, in the last couple of years political news and advocacy pages have sprung up on platforms like Facebook (see Herrman 2016). What is unique about these media outlets is the fact that they do not exist outside of social media sites, but nevertheless attract a significant audience. They are based on algorithms, which filter and sort the content "to show people what is most relevant to them" (Adamic, Bakshy, and Messing 2015). Here the homophilic mechanism shows through, because the content, which is aggregated from a multiplicity of sources, is sifted according to the preferences of the user—or at least according to what the algorithm thinks these preferences could be. Hence, the idea of topicality, central to mass media logic, is being subverted: instead of bringing everyone up-to-date with the same information, different stories circulate in different parts of the network, and by sharing them in peer groups, existing opinions get confirmed, while deviant opinions are filtered out. Such a confirmation bias, well known in psychology, has profound implications for a common space of reference:

> While it may seem that the decline of symbolic efficiency ushers in a new era of freedom from rigid norms and expectations, the fluidity and adaptability of imaginary identities are accompanied by fragility and insecurity. Imaginary identities are incapable of establishing a firm place to stand, a position from which one can make sense of one's experiences, one's worlds. (Dean 2010, 57)

As Jodi Dean points out, to pin down meaning is getting more and more difficult with social media, where the truth becomes a matter of perception, rather than the result of intersubjectively agreed-upon facts.

The internet has created a new desire for participation, but other than the participatory hopes of the 1990s, the will to participate doesn't seem to yield a common space of reference anymore. In a world in which every opinion can be expressed, paranoia penetrates almost all aspects of our lives, which, in turn, has dramatic effects on the understanding of a participatory public sphere (see Chun 2006). The result can be seen in recent political debates, where exaggeration, suspicion, and conspiratorial fantasies continuously spill over into the discourse: if I lose, the elections are rigged; only the polls in my favor are trustworthy; all the others are part of a conspiracy against me. This reemergence of a "paranoid style in politics" (see Hofstadter 1964) is possible due to the aforementioned postfact situation. And even if such a situation was already immanent in European fascism at the beginning of the twentieth century or the McCarthy-era in the United States, it is gaining significant momentum at a time when data simply outnum-

bers facts. Hence, the paranoid trait gets propelled by the fact that
there are no facts, or, to be more precise, only factitious facts.

Data–Information–Knowledge

In modern times, democratic debate has been dependent on so-
called expert knowledge, although it has always been clear that
such knowledge is itself dependent on the actual public opinion
of a given time. In this sense, the symbolic order prestructures
the condition of possibility of what can and cannot be expressed,
which, in retrospect, stabilizes the very same order. Even fascism
tried to enshrine its grotesque and death-dealing laws in a fact-
based scientific discourse, not only to prove its alleged superiority
but also to justify its crimes. The dispute over what counts as a fact
and what does not was at the very core of modern "games of truth"
(see Foucault 1984, 386–88). Today, by contrast, the effort to maintain at least a pretense of truth, which is based on facts, seems no
longer to be of importance. As can be seen with recent events, such
as the Brexit, Trumpism, and the notorious and tiring prevarication
of the European far right, to tell a lie, and being caught doing so, is
no longer a cause for embarrassment. It seems that white men's
discourse does not rely on expertise, however botchy it might be,
in order to insist on being right. All that is needed is some poorly
researched information: £350m supposedly sent to the EU every
week by Downing Street, increasing crime rates caused by refugees
in the United States and Germany alike—all of these are simple
lies, but do not stain the reputations of those who tell them. On
the contrary, they may not speak the truth but are nonetheless
beloved by a significant part of the population who sympathize
with their authoritarian view; even more so, because they are
believed to stand their ground against all those academic wiseacres
and pundits.

If hermeneutics is considered to be the art of differentiation between bullshit and facts, then the question arises as to why it is not
central to the exercise of power anymore? Why can we endlessly

produce evidence to counter obvious lies, and no one really seems to care? This is the implicit question of Hito Steyerl's contribution in this volume. She explains how "probability enters truth production on an extensive scale" (Steyerl in this volume). Rather than facts, which need to be verified by some sort of institution, data, which is endlessly processed and filtered, constitutes the basis of truthfulness today; with the effect "that the patterns supposed to be uncovered in massive data correspond to some degree with the patterns that are already assumed to be found there" (Steyerl). In other words: what we are looking for is not so much veracity, built on traditional inquiry and reasoning, but opinions and beliefs that fit into our world views. As a consequence, the age of facts and truth finding is being replaced by a new era, characterized by a permissive and incessant interpretation of data (see Lepore 2016).[8]

Of course, one could ask, why bother with the truth anyway? Wasn't it the intrinsic goal of postmodern critique to get rid of or at least destabilize the grand narratives of modernity? Why becoming sissy, when Trump, Le Pen, or Strache are mocking the mainstream opinion of being biased itself? Well, because a common understanding of what is true, and what is not true, is important for the constitution of an objective reality, that is, a reality based on intersubjectively negotiated norms and rules. If such an agreement is annulled or simply ignored, society as a whole runs the risk of becoming cynical about its own truth and therefore existence. Again, none of this is new.[9] However, with the rise of Big Data, we have reached a new qualitative step of soothsaying. The constant growth of data makes the idea of evidence-based politics appear outdated, because data, by definition, can be interpreted in this or that way. There is no major event that isn't entangled in a web of assertions and objections. No news not chopped up and distributed via social media channels, to the effect that a common space of cultural, social, and political reference is being rendered impossible. Due to this process, accelerated by personalized and personalizing algorithms, we risk missing the big picture for our small echo chambers filled with personal data (see Pariser 2012).

It is in the light of such a "data overflow" that Hito Steyerl discusses the implications of pattern recognition. In order to distinguish signal from noise, people always relied on specific patterns. In this context, racist and sexist algorithmic cultures are not so different from Ancient Greece, when women and slaves were barred—or should we say, filtered—from the public discourse. Their voices were not heard, because they did not apply to the specific set of values in the Greek polis. They may have been quantitatively significant, but they were not qualitatively relevant. Data, in the sense of a given thing (lat. *datum*), needs to be processed, in order to obtain meaning. Or, more simply, it needs to be put into form (lat. *informare*). Hence, a deliberate act is required, whereby data is applied to a preexisting scheme or pattern.[10] And this process, as Hito Steyerl points out in this volume, is a "fundamentally political operation." By applying filters, we constantly (re-)create them, particularly since the act of filtering information from data lies at the very heart of how we create our world.

Put into psychoanalytical and, in particular, Lacanian terms, one could say that unfiltered data represents the real, the absolute unknowable, whereas information stands for reality, rendered intelligible by our cognitive filters. Reality, in turn, can be seen as a composite of the imaginary and the symbolic, the two registers responsible for the constitution of our self.[11] Thus, looking at the example of Google's Deep Dream Generator from Steyerl's text, we can see how the algorithmic training of an artificial neural network, which is constituted by a large amount of data, ends up by overidentifying with its own training set. Like humans are haunted by the demons of the past in their dreams, the algorithms, while trying to filter intelligible information from the noise of the deep web, simply repeat the imaginary they were fed with. "But"—and this is crucial in Steyerl's analysis—"in a very materialist sense, these entities are far from hallucinations. If they are dreams, those dreams can be interpreted as condensations or displacements of the current technological disposition." What we see in the phantasmagoric creatures is what Google offers us: its unleashed prosumerist vision of "corporate animism in which commodities are not only fetishes but dreamed-up, franchised chimeras" (Steyerl). The produced signals are not just some dreamed-up images but representations of our current techno-capitalist system.

Now the crux of the matter is that dreams are not facts, and that Google is not (yet) equivalent to our reality. In fact, the latter is not only constituted by the imaginary but also by the symbolic. A tech company may be very influential when it comes to the imagination of our future, but it is only one player, albeit a powerful one, In the social deliberation of intersubjectively accepted patterns and codes. This leads us to knowledge as a third layer of analysis: in addition to data and information,[12] knowledge can be seen as an agreed-upon framework for evaluating experiences and information. Take the example of the weather forecast: the measuring instruments of a meteorological station produce data in the form of discrete units. This array of figures, let's say numbers from 0 to 9, only becomes legible when being applied to a specific scheme like the Celsius scale, a task normally done by experts. But in order to both make sense to the public and be accepted by it, this information has to be presented within a context that pins down meaning and gives it relevance. This is why people across the globe still watch the weather forecast every evening at a given time, or consult their most trusted app to show them the predicted temperature for the next day. This shared symbolic realm is necessary for information to be considered reliable.[13]

While hallucinations take place at the imaginary level, and thus are only accessible to the individual, delusions refer to the symbolic, in which we rely on agreed-upon norms and values. This is why a distortion of reality can also happen collectively, in the sense that a social group deviates from common sense and its understanding of what is true and what is false. As theories of radical democracy have shown, these deviations are even intrinsic to the political process, because social reality is always in the making (see Laclau and Mouffe 2001). By the same token, we can never be sure whether the reality we live in isn't delusional itself. There are no generalizable criteria to determine its veracity, because every time we try, we are thrown back to reality. Conversely, to call another symbolic order delusional is only possible based on the prerequisite of an already established order, from which the alleged delusion is distinguished (see Foucault 1988). So our collectively agreed-upon reality provides us with a set of beliefs, ideas, and norms, which serve as a point of reference.

In accordance with Michel Serres's idea of the excluded third, this common sense needs to be hidden in order to be effective. An essential part of hegemonic power, therefore, entails the ability to render deviant visions of the world impossible, while presenting the "real world" as the only possible one. This, in particular, is true about tech companies, whose imaginary is deeply rooted in the idea that their products are created to improve the world and our lives. Yet, what they do come up with are cock-and-bull stories, which, with the aid of massive advertising budgets, are sold to the public in order to become part of our everyday version of reality. Think about cloud computing, for example. The idea that some cloud is a trustworthy place for all our data, from holiday pics to our health information to our secret desires and wishes, is not only puzzling but profoundly problematic. And still, we use cloud storage services, even if we should and actually do know better. "I think conspiracy and paranoia are just what the cloud needs," explains Tung-Hui Hu, the author of *A Prehistory of the Cloud,* because "the system works like a massive pyramid scheme—we all need to believe that it's everywhere in order for it to be everywhere" (Sutcliffe 2015). This delusional drive lies at the very root of digital cultures and how they have unfolded over the last decades.

Pattern Recognition

In a review of William Gibson's 2003 novel *Pattern Recognition,* Fredric Jameson calls the collective unconscious of global consumerism the "eBay Imaginary" (see Jameson 2003), a notion that, fifteen years later, can be extended to Apple, Amazon, Facebook, Google, and Microsoft. The so-called "Big Five" of the internet do not only constitute the backbone of today's platform capitalism but are also at the forefront of predicting our techno-cultural future. In fact, the ability to identify potential trends from vast amounts of data, or, even better, to create them in the first place, has become the lifeline of capitalist production, with the effect that companies are contingent on new modes of pattern recognition that allow them to read the future. Now for Jameson, the breathtaking development in information and communication technologies refers to the most recent push for modernization, best represented by Gibson's "high-tech paranoia," in which "the circuits and networks of some putative global computer hookup are narratively mobilized by labyrinthine conspiracies of autonomous but deadly interlocking and competing information agencies in a complexity often beyond the capacity of the normal reading mind" (Jameson 1991, 38). In the postmodern world, the individual gets lost in the hyper-space of computer networks. Not only does she lose her ability to locate herself within this space, but she is also dispersed into a myriad of datasets.

While Jameson associates cyberpunk's "high-tech paranoia" with individual anxiety, social conspiracies, and the annihilation of the self, which is the pathological sediment of postmodern society, others have stressed the liberating effects arising from a destabilization of the modern subject and its totalizing master narratives (see Lyotard 1979; Deleuze and Guattari 1983; Vattimo 1988; Holmes 2009). In particular, Félix Guattari calls for new "collective assemblages of enunciation" (Guattari 1996, 263) in order to overcome the normative subjectivity of mass-mediated publics.[14] This pluralistic approach not only challenges the idea of the individual in its singularity but was indeed seen as an immanent process of becoming a collective, which itself should be experienced as a process of greater freedom. In our "post-media era" (see Guattari 2013), the collective appropriation and use of media technologies by a multitude of "subject-groups" (Guattari 2000, 60) nourished the hopes that new modes of subjectivation would emerge, able to break through the mind-numbing effects of mass media.

However, the deconstruction of mass-mediated subjectivity poses the aforementioned problem that a common space of reference, within which you can agree or disagree, is increasingly difficult to maintain.

The transition from mass media to social media corresponds with Guattari's prospect of post-(mass)mediality. The desired liberation and multiplication of the subject has lead to a new imaginary of participation. But other than the hoped-for resingularization— that is the ability of individuals to collectively remap their world—Info-capitalism has managed to retain the old model of exploitation by adjusting it to the new conditions of data production. Instead of a common vision that "designates an investment of attention, libidinal energy, and time," what "happens today on Facebook, Twitter, and the like, is the reverse, which in spite of being the virtual home of a truly massive ensemble of humans, never form a collective project of 'being-together'" (Hui and Halpin 2013, 107). In social media, the individual gets atomized, in order to become a source of data production, as well as an identifiable subject for marketing. This form of algorithmic governance is well known by now. However, most of today's critical examination is simply repeating the implicit presuppositions of the problem, that is that the individual has to be preserved, rather than asking for new forms of individuation in our postmedia time. Such an approach doesn't necessarily imply an affirmation of the status quo; on the contrary, it could help to set up some criteria to better understand, and maybe even vanquish the paranoid anxiety caused by "postmodern confusion" (see Chun 2015).

There is, of course, no clear-cut definition of what paranoia actually is. In its colloquial use, the term often gets confused with delusional disorder in the broader sense of the word (see Jaspers 1997) or the rather clinical schizophrenia (see Bleuler 1912). However, if we want to understand some of the specific aspects of paranoia, we can start with its etymology: The word *paranoia* is a composition of the Greek words παρά (*para*), meaning "beside, next," and νόος (*noos*), that is "mind"; so paranoia literally translates into "being next to your mind." This seems to be consistent, given that the term is still used to describe a mental state of delusional or "false" belief regarding the self or persons or objects outside the self that is maintained despite indisputable evidence to the contrary.[15] In this sense, paranoia can be seen as a partial, subordinate aspect of a delusion disorder; were it not for the fact that the French word for delusion, *délire,* stems from the Latin word *delirium,* which means "to go off the furrow" and, therefore, is almost equivalent with paranoia in the sense of "being deranged or distorted."[16] Even more, the German word *Wahn* or *wähnen,* which descends from the Indo-European *wen,* has the same root as in "to win," and can be taken to mean "to imagine" and "to believe," but also "to search," "to strive," or "to hope for something." This is a crucial point in defining the delusional trait, in particular because it refers to a productive, if not salutary and reparative aspect in what we usually dismiss as paranoia disorder.[17]

Paranoia as a specific way of knowing things is, along these lines, not so much caused by a lack of information as by an overproduction of meaning.[18] Following the canonic description by German neurologist and psychiatrist Klaus Conrad, we can define a delusional episode on the basis of—at least—three stages (see Conrad 1958):[19] First, there is the *trema (Wahnstimmung),* a delusional atmosphere, comparable to stage fright. You know that something is going on, but you cannot figure out what it is. This mental condition is associated with the sensation of suspiciousness, alienation, and fear, but also an anticipatory excitement. Second, the moment of revelation, termed *apophenia (Wahnwahrnehmung),* when things start to make sense again. Apophenia is described here as the spontaneous perception of connections and meaningfulness, accompanied by a triumphant sentiment of having discovered something of tremendous significance. Such an Aha! moment is central to the paranoid perception of the world. And third, *anastrophe (Wahneinfall),* that is the delusional state of irreversible reference. Not only do things make sense to me, but they also begin to revolve around myself. Pathologically speaking, this is the point of no return, a "Copernican revolution" (Conrad), after which the delusional idea becomes solid and incorrigible. Put into an even more simple model, we can speak of only two stages in the development of a delusion disorder: first the collapse of a central symbolic order, triggering the delusional sensation of the trema; and then the attempt to restore such an order by the discovery and, ultimately, ossification of a delusional idea, which helps to reconstitute the world (Kupke 2012, 116). In fact, the paranoid desire can be seen as a self-healing mechanism, a protective function to reappropriate the world.

It is not by chance that in cultural history and theory, media technologies often pop up as objects of desire of delusional systems: from telegraphy, to radio, to the internet (see Kittler 1984; Stingelin 1989; Chun 2006). Human cognition has always been embedded in media-technological environments, but it is with the rise of digital media that the need to develop a systematic understanding of our technologically modulated environments has become vital (see Hörl 2015). The concept of paranoia can be a useful tool in this context, because it helps to uncover societal beliefs, which have to be hidden, in order to function properly.[20] The paranoid person draws on the same beliefs, with the significant difference being that he or she overaffirms, and, thereby, reveals them. Hence, the irony behind pattern recognition algorithms like Google's Deep Dream Generator, analyzed by Hito Steyerl in this volume. It is a perfect example of an artificial neural network, which, by overidentifying with its own training set, becomes paranoid and, in doing so, gives us an insight into its inner functioning. What should be hidden behind the colorful curtain of Google's marketing department, unintentionally enters the stage, and what we see there is merely the fact that all the high-tech gimmicks are ultimately a reflection of techno-capitalism itself (see Steyerl).

Paranoid Thinking Machine

Germany, fall 2018: Three years after Angela Merkel's world-famous "We will manage," regarding Europe's so-called refugee crisis, the initial welcome culture has turned into a refusal culture. With the entry of the openly xenophobic and not-so-hidden racist Alternative for Germany (AfD) into the Bundestag, the political debate in Germany has become harsher, setting the tone for an unprecedented explosion of hate speech in social media, and, even worse, legitimizing physical violence and terrorist attacks against refugees.[21] What we are witnessing here are symptoms of a political crisis, namely the erosion of solidarity in society. Hate speech, therefore, needs to be seen as an alarming sign for the disintegration of a common public sphere, which, until now, served as the minimal framework for social negotiation processes. The inflammatory term "*Lügenpresse*" (lying press), popular among reactionary right-wing groups, points to a rupture in the political discourse: even if modern mass media (press, radio, TV) were always suspected of manipulating the public, their function as a general framework of reference, manipulative or not, was largely undisputed. With digital media, by contrast, we find ourselves in an imaginary of participation, in a world of images and affects, which leads to a dispersion of a common ground.[22]

Today's oppositional politics, in particular of the far right, is not so much concerned with the creation of a counterpublic, which sets itself to correct the reality produced by mainstream media, but rather with the creation of its own media and, therefore, its own truth. Blogs, online magazines and Facebook sites of right-wing populists in Europe, but also the alt-right movement in the United States, are manifestations of the aforementioned transition from mass media to social media logic. The *deadly* force of this transformation results from the fact that every withdrawal, total or partial, from the collectively shared realm of the social world triggers the collapse of the symbolic, which, in turn, leads to a further drifting apart of this world. However, the question remains whether this is simply a relentless demise, or if we need to develop "new attentional forms that pursue in a different manner the process of psychic and collective individuation" (Stiegler 2012). To break from the echo chambers of personalized data, we need to deploy the paranoid moment: while today's everyday media life is characterized by an excess of truth claiming, with the effect that the individual is caught in his or her own network, paranoia in its productive and salutary effects, may provide a stencil to redraw a symbolic order in our postmedia world.

A paranoid thinking machine, understood as a theoretical concept,[23] tries to compensate the symbolic void by filling it with meaning. The fact that these compensation efforts are currently characterized by hate speech reinforces the assumption that we are dealing with a social crisis of de-solidarization. But what if such a machine is put to different ends? What has to be done to switch the mode from hate to love? As Kübra Gümüşay reminded us at *re:publica* in May 2016, the hate against minorities in social media is highly organized, and, therefore, the only way to counter it is to organize love as well. This may sound naive but in fact points to the heart of what participation is all about: it is not only the act or state of having part of something, in order to be able to express your opinion, but also of sharing something in common, of becoming "an instance of a collective, not just one individual among others, but the very thing itself" (Kelty 2016, 236). This is why a debate about the reconstitution of a common symbolic order is so crucial; neither as a return to mass-media, nor as a "final" solution, but rather as a constant revision of the (post-)modern paradox that individuals are solicited by a collective will to share, and, by the same token, are thrown back into segregation.[24] As long as this debate isn't taking place, antiharassment tools, such as the ones recently introduced by Twitter and Instagram, can provide a first remedy to filter out the noise of racist and sexist slurs. And initiatives like TrollBusters, a platform to analyze and map how networks of harassers operate, are a good tactical means to fight back against hate speech. But in the long run, what we need is a strategy to reorganize our sociotechnical world, so that everyone feels free and safe to express him- and, in particular, herself.

In order to achieve this goal, or at least advance toward it, media, artistic, and cultural practices can be used to reflect on but also test the reconstitution of a common space of reference. While the imaginary of the digital is still caught in the neo-feudal ideology of platform capitalism, with its belief in individualist consumerism and reductive identity politics, only collective practices promise the creation of new attentional forms, which, in turn, could help to reassemble the paranoid thinking machine. This is not to claim that we can get rid of discrimination by simply invoking creative forms of enunciation. As has been argued throughout this book, pattern discrimination—that is, the ability to filter information from data—Is an essential part of human, but also nonhuman, cognition. However, what is at stake is the question of how and to what extent these patterns are themselves built on racist, sexist, and classist beliefs? Such a critical approach is sensible of the fact that the technological world functions as the excluded third, a world, which builds the basis for an increasing number of decision-making processes, and, therefore, needs to be brought into social and political awareness.

Notes

1   Slavoj Žižek refers to the concept of radical democracy (see Laclau and Mouffe 2001), in order to answer the "crucial question of the theory of ideology: the multitude of 'floating signifiers,' of protoideological elements, is structured into a unified field through the intervention of a certain 'nodal point' (the Lacanian *point de capiton*) which 'quilts' them, stops their sliding and fixes their meaning" (Žižek 2008, 95).

2   After the first three paradigms in scientific research, which were experimental, theoretical, and computational, the fourth paradigm indicates the analysis of massive data sets.

3   This adds another narcissistic wound to the human subject: After Copernicus's death blow to heliocentric cosmology, Darwin's dethroning of the human being, and Freud's subversion of the thinking subject, Big Data wrests the communication process from an anthropocentric worldview.

4   Actually this is the strategy of so-called "Reichsbürger" in Germany, who do not acknowledge the FRG to be a legitimate state. By painstakingly interpreting every legal document and executive order, they block any interaction with its institution.

5   Here Dean follows Slavoj Žižek's diagnosis of a demise of "symbolic efficiency" (Žižek 2000, 248).

6   See Cramer in this volume.

7   To be clear, by using the notion of the public sphere I am not following the

Habermasian idea of an ideal space that now disintegrates under the influence of networked media. On the contrary, this space has always already been a contested one, a hegemonial but necessary construction to constitute political subjects (Laclau and Mouffe 2001, xvii–xviii).

8   Michael P. Lynch, in his book *The Internet of Us,* speaks of "Google-Knowing" in this context (Lynch 2016, 21–40).

9   Friedrich Nietzsche already explained at length how human beings are constantly deceiving themselves in order to be able to survive. However, the salient but often overlooked point is that, precisely because of the artificiality of truth, humans have to believe in and take responsibility for it. In other words: Simply because facts are factitious doesn't mean they are of a nonbinding nature.

10 Think about the scheme, institutionalized by Greenwich Mean Time. The hands on your clock do not bear any meaning by themselves; in fact, they are just two (or three) mechanically (or digitally) driven pointers. Only when applied to the overall scheme of GMT can they tell you the time.

11 For a more systematic distinction between *the real* and *reality,* see Lacan's Seminar XI (Lacan 1977).

12 In information science, the relationship between data, information, knowledge, and sometimes wisdom is represented under the acronym DIKW.

13 The weather forecast also gives us an example of how we could deal with a postfact world: we normally accept the fact that the forecast, based on data from a wide range of sensory devices, only gives us a rough approximation of what will happen in the near future. No one would come up with the idea of holding the weather service accountable for possible mistakes. Even the usual complaints about the inaccuracy of the weather report are part of the narrative, which, and this is the salient point, is a common narrative.

14 Autonomous radio stations of the 1970s and 1980s in Europe (e.g., Radio Alice in Bologna) represented for Guattari an example of how collective assemblages of enunciation can be produced and preserved.

15 Typically manifested in delusions of persecution or grandeur that are often tantamount to paranoia. But as I want to argue here, paranoia is a much broader concept, referring to a feeling of radical insecurity due to a disorder of the symbolic system. Such an obscure feeling is often more difficult to endure than the belief of someone following.

16 Thanks to Wolfgang Sützl for literally spelling this out for me.

17 For the idea of a "reparative motive" in paranoid thinking, see Eve Kosofsky Sedgwick (2003).

18 See for example the work of Mark Lombardi, whose drawings meticulously document various topographies of political and financial power structures.

19 In fact, Conrad, a former member of the National Socialist German Physicians' League (NSDÄB) who also published on the heritability of epilepsy, differentiates between *trema, apophenia,* and *apocalypse,* whereas *anastrophe* works at the interface between the apophenic and apocalyptic phase. In this sense a catatonic psychosis is to be seen "one level lower" of the apophenic experience and is characterized by a sudden turnover into a stable delusional perception

(Conrad 1958, 192). However—for the sake of the argument—I am more interested in the actual "turning point" (lat. *crisis*) in order to understand the creative potential of paranoia (Schödlbauer 2016, 123).

20   See beginning of this text.

21   To be clear, the verbal and physical violence is, of course, also affecting non-refugees, not least Germans, who, due to a nationalist (*völkisch*) understanding of citizenship, are not considered to be "true" Germans. Unfortunately mainstream media is fueling this racist discourse, by repeatedly reporting on "*Ausländerfeindlichkeit*" (hostility to foreigners), even if the victims are Germans.

22   This can also be seen in the rise of a technocratic language to subvert such a common ground. Eighty years after Golda Meir's absolute despair in the face of a failing Évian Conference, during which the fate of more than half a million Jewish refugees was decided, Europe's heads of state and government are again merely speaking of "numbers" instead of human beings.

23   The idea for such a concept emerged from a conversation with Brian Holmes. My gratitude goes to him for his intellectual support.

24   See Chun in this volume.

References

Adamic, Lada, Eytan Bakshy, and Solomon Messing. 2015. "Exposure to Diverse Information on Facebook." *Facebook Research Blog,* May 7. Accessed December 21, 2016. https://research.fb.com/exposure-to-diverse-information-on-facebook-2.

Anderson, Chris. 2008. "The End of Theory: The Data Deluge Makes the Scientific Method Obsolete." *Wired*. Accessed December 21, 2016. https://www.wired.com/2008/06/pb-theory.

Beyes, Timon, and Claus Pias. 2016. "Transparency and Secrecy." In *Non-Knowledge and Digital Cultures,* Symposium, January 26–27. Accessed December 21, 2016. https://vimeo.com/165703739.

Bleuler, Eugen. 1912. *The Theory of Schizophrenic Negativism*, translated by William A. White. New York: The Journal of Nervous and Mental Disease Publishing Company.

Builder, Carl H. 1993. "Is It a Transition or a Revolution?" *Futures* 25:155–68.

Chun, Wendy Hui Kyong. 2006. *Control and Freedom: Power and Paranoia in the Age of Fiber Optics*. Cambridge, Mass.: MIT Press.

Chun, Wendy Hui Kyong. 2015. "Networks NOW: Belated Too Early." In *Postdigital Aesthetics: Art, Computation, and Design,* ed. David M. Berry and Michael Dieter, 289–315. London: Palgrave Macmillan.

Chun, Wendy Hui Kyong. 2016. *Updating to Remain the Same: Habitual New Media.* Cambridge, Mass.: MIT Press.

Conrad, Klaus. 1958. *Die beginnende Schizophrenie: Versuch einer Gestaltanalyse des Wahns.* Stuttgart: G. Thieme.

Dean, Jodi. 2010. *Blog Theory: Feedback and Capture in the Circuits of Drive*. Cambridge: Polity Press.

Deleuze, Gilles, and Félix Guattari. 1983. *Anti-Oedipus: Capitalism and Schizophrenia,* trans. Robert Hurley, Mark Seem, and Helen R. Lane. Minneapolis: University of Minnesota Press.

Dijck, José van, and Thomas Poell. 2013. "Understanding Social Media Logic." *Media and Communication* 1, no. 1: 2–14.

Foucault, Michel. 1984. "Polemics, Politics, and Problematizations." In *The Foucault Reader,* ed. Paul Rabinow, 381–90. New York: Pantheon Books.

Foucault, Michel. 1988. *Madness and Civilization: A History of Insanity in the Age of Reason,* trans. Richard Howard. New York: Vintage Books.

Groys, Boris. 2012. *Under Suspicion: A Phenomenology of Media,* trans. Carsten Strathausen. New York: Columbia University Press.

Guattari, Félix. 1996. "Remaking Social Practices." In *The Guattari Reader,* ed. Gary Genosko, 262–72. Oxford: Blackwell.

Guattari, Félix. 2000. *The Three Ecologies,* trans. Ian Pindar and Paul Sutton. London: The Athlone Press.

Guattari, Félix. 2013. "Towards a Post-Media Era." In *Provocative Alloys: A Post-Media Anthology,* ed. Clemens Apprich et al., 26–27. London: Mute.

Habermas, Jürgen. 1989. *The Structural Transformation of the Public Sphere,* trans. Thomas Burger and Frederick Lawrence. Cambridge, Mass.: MIT Press.

Hagen, Wolfgang. 2016. "Discharged Crowds: On the Crisis of a Concept." In *Social Media—New Masses,* ed. Inge Baxmann, Timon Beyes, and Claus Pias, 123–34. Zurich: diaphanes.

Hall, Stuart. 1999. "Encoding, Decoding." In *The Cultural Studies Reader,* ed. Simon During, 507–17. London: Routledge.

Harari, José V., and David F. Bell. 1982. "Introduction : Journal à plusieurs votes." In *Michel Serres: Hermes: Literature, Science, Philosophy,* ed. José V. Harari and David F. Bell, ix–xl. Baltimore: The John Hopkins University Press.

Herrman, John. 2016. "Inside Facebook's (Totally Insane, Unintentionally Gigantic, Hyperpartisan) Political-Media Machine: How a Strange New Class of Media Outlet Has Arisen to Take Over Our News Feeds." *New York Times,* August 24. Accessed December 21, 2016. http://www.nytimes.com/2016/08/28/magazine/inside -facebooks-totally-insane-unintentionally-gigantic-hyperpartisan-political-media -machine.html?_r=1.

Hey, Tony, Stewart Tansley, and Kristin Tolle. 2009. *The Fourth Paradigm: Data-Intensive Scientific Discovery.* Redmond: Microsoft Research.

Hörl, Erich. 2015. "The Technological Condition," trans. Anthony Enns. *Parrhesia* 22:1–15.

Hofstadter, Richard. 1964. "The Paranoid Style in American Politics." *Harper's Magazine,* November. Accessed December 21, 2016. http://harpers.org/archive/1964/ 11/the-paranoid-style-in-american-politics.

Holmes, Brian. 2009. *Escape the Overcode: Activist Art in the Control Society.* Zagreb: WHW/Eindhoven: Abbemuseum.

Hui, Yuk, and Harry Halpin. 2013. "Collective Individuation: The Future of the Social Web." In *Unlike Us Reader: Social Media Monopolies and Their Alternatives,* ed. Geert Lovink and Miriam Rasch, 103–16. Amsterdam: INC.

122 Jameson, Fredric. 1991. *Postmodernism, or, the Cultural Logic of Late Capitalism*. Durham, N.C.: Duke University Press.

Jameson, Fredric. 2003. "Fear and Loathing in Globalization." *New Left Review*, September-October. Accessed December 21, 2016. https://newleftreview.org/II/23/fredric-jameson-fear-and-loathing-in-globalization.

Jaspers, Karl. 1997 (1913). *General Psychopathology*, trans. J. Hoenig and Marian W. Hamilton. Baltimore: The John Hopkins University Press.

Kelty, Christopher. 2016. "Participation." In *Digital Keywords: A Vocabulary of Information Society & Culture,* ed. Benjamin Peters, 227–40. Princeton, N.J.: Princeton University Press.

Kittler, Friedrich A. 1984. "Flechsig/Schreber/Freud: Ein Nachrichtennetzwerk der Jahrhundertwende." *Der Wunderblock: Zeitschrift für Psychoanalyse* 11/12:56–68.

Kupke, Christian. 2012. "Von der symbolischen Ordnung des Wahns zum Wahn der symbolischen Ordnung: Ein vorläufiger philosophischer Versuch." In *Wahn: Philosophische, psychoanalytische und kulturwissenschaftliche Perspektiven*, ed. Gerhard Unterthurner and Ulrike Kadi, 107–36. Vienna and Berlin: Turia + Kant.

Lacan, Jacques. 1977. *The Seminar of Jacques Lacan: The Four Fundamental Concepts of Psychoanalysis*, ed Jacques-Alain Miller, trans. Alan Sheridan. New York: W. W. Norton.

Laclau, Ernesto, and Chantal Mouffe. 2001. *Hegemony and Socialist Strategy. Towards a Radical Democratic Politics*, London: Verso.

Lepore, Jill. 2016. "After the Fact: In the History of Truth, a New Chapter Begins." *The New Yorker*, March 21. Accessed December 21, 2016. http://www.newyorker.com/magazine/2016/03/21/the-internet-of-us-and-the-end-of-facts.

Luhmann, Niklas. 2000. *The Reality of Mass Media*, trans. Kathleen Cross. Stanford, Calif.: Stanford University Press.

Lynch, Michael P. 2016. *The Internet of Us: Knowing More and Understanding Less in the Age of Big Data*. New York: W. W. Norton.

Lyotard, Jean-François. 1979. *La condition postmoderne: rapport sur le savoir*. Paris: Minuit.

Nietzsche, Friedrich. 1989. "On Truth and Lying in an Extra-Moral Sense (1873)." In *Friedrich Nietzsche on Rhetoric and Language*, ed. and trans. Sander L. Gilman, Carole Blair, and David J. Parent, 246–57. New York: Oxford University Press.

Pariser, Eli. 2012. *The Filter Bubble: How the New Personalized Web Is Changing What We Read and How We Think*. New York: Penguin Random House.

Pias, Claus. 2002. "Der Hacker." In *Grenzverletzer: Figuren politischer Subversion,* ed. Eva Horn and Stefan Kaufmann, 248–70. Berlin: Kadmos. Accessed December 21, 2016. https://www.uni-due.de/~bj0063/texte/hacker.pdf.

Ricoeur, Paul. 1970. *Freud and Philosophy: An Essay on Interpretation*. New Haven, Conn.: Yale University Press.

Schleiermacher, Friedrich. 1998. *Hermeneutics and Criticism and Other Writings*, trans. Andrew Bowie. Cambridge: Cambridge University Press.

Schödlbauer, Michael. 2016. *Wahnbegegnungen: Zugänge zur Paranoia*. Köln: Psychiatrie Verlag.

Serres, Michel. 1982. *Hermes: Literature, Science, Philosophy*, ed. José V. Harari and David F. Bell. Baltimore: The John Hopkins University Press.

Sedgwick, Eve Kosofsky. 2003. "Paranoid Reading and Reparative Reading, or, You're So Paranoid, You Probably Think This Essay Is About You." In *Touching Feeling: Affect, Pedagogy, Performativity*, 123–51. Durham, N.C.: Duke University Press.

Stiegler, Bernard. 2012. "Relational Ecology and The Digital *Pharmakon*." *Culture Machine* 13. Accessed December 21, 2016. https://www.culturemachine.net/index .php/cm/article/viewArticle/464.

Stingelin, Martin. 1989. "Gehirntelegraphie: Die Rede der Paranoia von der Macht der Medien um 1900. Falldarstellungen." In *Arsenale der Seele. Literatur- und Medienanalyse seit 1870,* ed. Friedrich A. Kittler and Georg Christoph Tholen, 51–70. Munich: Wilhelm Fink Verlag, 1989.

Sutcliffe, Jamie. 2015. "A Prehistory of The Cloud: An Interview with Tung-Hui Hu." *Rhizome*, December 16. Accessed December 21, 2016. http://rhizome.org/editorial /2015/dec/16/interview-tung-hui-hu.

Varnelis, Kazys, ed. 2008. *Networked Publics*. Cambridge, Mass.: MIT Press.

Vattimo, Gianni. 1988. *The End of Modernity: Nihilism and Hermeneutics in Postmodern Culture,* trans. Jon R. Snyder. Cambridge: Polity Press.

Žižek, Slavoj. 2000. *The Ticklish Subject*. London: Verso.

Žižek, Slavoj. 2008. *The Sublime Object of Ideology*. London: Verso.

Authors

Clemens Apprich is visiting professor at the Institute of Culture and Aesthetics of Digital Media (ICAM), Leuphana University of Lüneburg. He is the author of *Technotopia: A Media Genealogy of Net Cultures.*

Wendy Hui Kyong Chun is Simon Fraser University's Canada 150 Research Chair in New Media in SFU School of Communication. She is the author of several books, including most recently *Updating to Remain the Same: Habitual New Media.*

Florian Cramer is reader in 21st Century Visual Culture at Willem de Kooning Academy in Rotterdam, Netherlands.

Hito Steyerl is professor of experimental film and video at the Berlin University of the Arts. She is the author of several books, including most recently *Duty Free Art: Art in the Age of Planetary Civil War.*